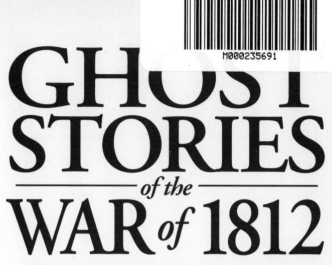

GHOST STORIES *of the* WAR *of* 1812

Haunted Spirits of Canada and the U.S.

Maria Da Silva & Andrew Hind

GHOST HOUSE

Ghost House Books

The Distributor: Lone Pine Publishing
2311 – 96 Street
Edmonton, AB T6N 1G3
Canada

Websites: www.ghostbooks.net
        www.lonepinepublishing.com

Library and Archives Canada Cataloguing in Publication

Da Silva, Maria
    Ghost stories of the War of 1812 / Maria da Silva and Andrew Hind.

ISBN 978-1-55105-889-4

    1. Canada--History--War of 1812. I. Hind, Andrew II. Title.

FC449.G4D2 2012   971.03'4   C2012-904761-9

Editorial Director: Nancy Foulds
Project Editor: Sheila Quinlan
Production Manager: Gene Longson
Layout and Production: Alesha Braitenbach
Cover Design: Gerry Dotto
Cover Images: photo of soldiers: © Jtlewis | Dreamstime.com; ghostly
smoke: © Thinkstock.com

Photography: All photos are by Andrew Hind and Maria Da Silva except:
pp. 26, 124, Niagara Historical Museum; pp. 35, 93, Parks Canada; p. 39,
Huronia Parks; pp. 194, 204, Sheila Gibbs; p. 200, Dennis Skipper; pp. 253,
258, Rebecca Pascoe.

We acknowledge the financial support of the Government of Canada
through the Canada Book Fund (CBF) for our publishing activities.

 Canadian   Patrimoine
Heritage   canadien

PC: 1

Contents

Dedication

This work is offered as a salute to the memory of the men on both sides who served, sacrificed and died as they loyally obeyed their country's call to arms in the War of 1812. It's also dedicated to the families they kissed and left behind, who often suffered as much—if in different ways—as the soldiers in the field.

Foreword

While many people associate ghost stories with tall tales and wildly imaginative yarns meant to frighten and chill, this book is not a work of fiction. It details true hauntings from across the continent, all of which are tied to the War of 1812. By true, we mean that every story in this volume has a strong tradition or historical foundation upon which to rest, and came from eyewitnesses who swore the experiences they recounted were factual—these stories are certainly true for those who reported them. While we cannot prove beyond the shadow of a doubt that any of these tales involve entities that somehow defy the supposedly one-way road souls take after death, they are not fictional accounts.

We also attempted to recount the experiences as told to us with little artistic licence. It's our belief that while ghost stories should be dramatic, they should also be truthfully presented and, as much as possible, authenticated. As a result, we extensively researched every story presented within this book using archival material, newspapers and interviews with knowledgeable individuals. The most strenuous efforts have been made for accuracy, both in historical detail and in the retelling of our sources' paranormal encounters.

While this book has been laid to rest (so to speak), our explorations of the strange and the mysterious have certainly not come to and end. We are always looking for further stories to add to our files. We would appreciate additional War of 1812 stories for a possible sequel to this book, but in truth any tale is of interest to us. If you know a haunting or unusual tale, or you have experienced something paranormal yourself, please contact us at either dasilvababy@hotmail.com (Maria Da Silva) or maelstrom@sympatico.ca (Andrew Hind). Please also visit our website: mariaandandrew.weebly.com.

In the meantime, enjoy the book. Just be sure to keep the lights on.

Introduction

The War of 1812 has the strange distinction of being largely forgotten by both of its main participants, and yet its outcome was critically important to the future of North America. The conflict, which lasted three terrible years, was a bloody confrontation that tore most of the continent, including the British colonies of Upper and Lower Canada (Ontario and Quebec, respectively), the American frontier and parts of the Atlantic coast and the Gulf of Mexico. The war saw British, American, Canadian and First Nations forces engage in vicious fighting in more than a dozen large battles and numerous skirmishes. Still, the War of 1812 tends to be overlooked and overshadowed.

As we write this book, however, the bicentennial of the war is upon us and interest is consequently growing. Awareness of this war and its important role in charting the course of Canada and the United States will undoubtedly increase as media and commemorative events on both sides of the border cast light upon it. That's a welcome development.

What better time, then, to explore the subject of ghosts of the War of 1812? And what better way to introduce readers to the story of the conflict than through the eyes—staring with undeath though they may now be—of ghostly participants in that conflict? Entertaining and educational, with a few good chills thrown in for good measure…that's what this book is all about.

From the northern shores of Lake Ontario to the Maine coast and as far south as New Orleans, there are as many ghost stories related to this conflict as there were battles and skirmishes 200 years past. The war gave rise to a rich tradition of tales, from spectral soldiers still locked in battle to this day and heroic generals cut down in the prime of their lives to wraith-like ships floating across the waves and women who wait for their lovers to return. *Ghost Stories of the War of 1812* is an eerie exploration of the phantom-filled battlefields and historic sites of this conflict. Drawn from both archival sources and first-hand accounts, the stories herein weave together anecdote, eyewitness accounts, history and folklore to form a rich tapestry depicting a rarely explored side of the War of 1812.

Why have so many of those who participated in the war risen from their graves to haunt a world that is no longer theirs? Extreme circumstances often lead to the formation of ghosts. Tales of unquiet battlefields filled with walking dead are common across the world and from every war. Lives cut short, the agony of terrible wounds, the fear of facing death...scenes of fighting are scarred by mass misery. It's hard to imagine a more terrifying and personal form of combat than that experienced by soldiers involved in the War of 1812.

The warfare of two centuries ago was brutal, dirty work. Unlike today's clinical and decimating aerial warfare, which looks like a video game when shown on television to the public watching from the safety of their couches, the battles of the War of 1812 were waged by musket-bearing soldiers in muddy fields and woods, the fighting up-close and personal. Men were formed into tight ranks and marched slowly, methodically, toward the enemy lines. Once they were within musket range, the officers would order a halt and the carnage would begin. When a man fired, he was showered with a spray of sparks and burning powder grains from the pan of his musket, which might scar his face or even set fire to his clothing, and he was nearly blinded by smoke; to prevent injury to their eyes, many men closed them when firing. Soldiers in the front rank were deafened by the weapons of the rear rank. Occasionally there would be an ominous whack as a musket ball hit home. The fallen soldier would be pulled clear of the firing line and left, his comrades forced to ignore his moans. Cannon balls would crash through the packed ranks, shattering limbs and severing heads from bodies as they cut their bloody swaths. You couldn't run, you couldn't hide, you couldn't even duck. All you could do was fire, reload and fire again as men fell all around and until such time as the commanding officer ordered a bayonet charge or a reluctant retreat to concede the battlefield. In this light, it's little wonder that many War of 1812 battlefields are haunted.

But we don't just find ghosts lingering where muskets rattled and cannons boomed, and not all restless spirits from that time were soldiers. The War of 1812 tore families apart, saw homes and even entire villages burned to the ground, separated lovers for years on end, led to widespread suffering and worry and destroyed men's reputations. In many cases, such emotional turmoil gave rise to departed souls who refuse to leave the realm of mortals, lingering in a state of boundless sorrow or deathless malice. We find homes haunted by ghostly women whose worlds were turned upside down, a former president and first lady lingering in the White House well past their term of office, murder victims seeking justice from the grave and betrothed couples seeking to reunite with one another. When we began researching this volume, we were surprised at the wide variety of dreadful tales to choose from. If you think the only ghosts from the War of 1812 are found on battlegrounds, think again.

Our own first experience with the psychic echoes of this conflict came years before we were even asked to write this book. While visiting the charming town of Niagara-on-the-Lake for a travel article, we happened to dine at the Olde Angel Inn, perhaps Ontario's oldest existing inn, dating back to the very early 19th century. While enjoying our meal, we learned from the attending waitress of the establishment's resident ghost, former British officer Captain Colin Swayze. His is a moving story: while his army retreated from the advancing Americans in 1813, he lingered behind to share a tearful goodbye and one last passionate kiss with his beloved, the daughter of the innkeeper. Unfortunately, he was discovered hiding in the basement by enemy soldiers, bayoneted to death, and buried beneath the earthen floor. Ever since, the inn has been inhabited by Swayze's mournful ghost. A fantastically sad and romantic story, we agreed, then went back to our food, ghosts and ill-fated loves soon forgotten.

Then we ventured down the creaking, age-worn stairs into the basement to use the restrooms and discovered that Swayze's ghost was far more than merely a tale told over a drink and alongside a roaring fire. Maria's hand was just above the handle when the door to the ladies room pulled open. She stepped back to allow space for the woman exiting to pass and was surprised when no one emerged. Shrugging her shoulders, Maria entered the ladies room, fully expecting to find someone else in there. The room was completely empty. Maria was now a little unnerved. How had the door opened by itself? She was pondering this question even as she began to feel that she wasn't entirely alone, as if she was being watched by unseen eyes. She hurried out of the washroom as quickly as possible, and later learned that many people have reported unusual happenings and eerie sensations there. Had the gentlemanly Captain Swayze tried to open the door for Maria? We like to think so.

The War of 1812 isn't ancient history. It's still very much alive, if only in the form of soldier apparitions for whom the conflict has never ended. Captain Swayze is far from alone. We discovered enough ghosts related to the War of 1812 to easily form a spectral army. For them, the war is not over at all. Their undead existence is an eternity of fear, loss, pain, anguish and hardship. For too long, the sacrifices of the men who fought and died for their respective countries during this war have been almost forgotten, overshadowed in the public memory by larger conflicts. With the coming of the bicentennial and numerous events on both sides of the border commemorating it, the War of 1812 is finally getting its due. Awareness and appreciation of the conflict, its causes and repercussions, and the men who fought in it is growing. That's a welcome development.

But does it mean souls made restless by the war will finally find peace? Don't hold your breath. Late at night, when clouds flee like dark shadows across the moon, when wispy tendrils of fog reach out to ensnare you and haunting, unidentifiable noises play upon the wind, the ghosts of the War of 1812 will crawl from their graves to stalk the night and renew their ceaseless battle.

Outline of a Ghastly War

Ghost Stories of the War of 1812 is, as the title suggests, a book about the supernatural. That said, most of the haunting stories herein involve, to some degree or another, battles and military campaigns. Without knowing the wider context in which these tales take place, it's difficult to fully appreciate or comprehend them. We knew we didn't want to bog readers down with too much extraneous historical detail within the stories themselves, but we also recognize that there is nothing more frustrating than having to put a book down to track down an unfamiliar reference.

Our solution was to include a chapter that relates, in brief but comprehensive detail, the path the War of 1812 took over three long years of fighting. Anyone who wishes to look elsewhere for greater detail on the battles, campaigns and personalities of the war is encouraged to do so, but for the casual reader this chapter should suffice to allow them to comprehend the course of the conflict and the ghost stories to which it gave birth. Of course, while we believe a general understanding of the war enhances one's appreciation of this book as a whole, those who have little interest in military history can feel free to skip this chapter.

The Road to War

The relationship between the United States and Britain had been cool ever since America earned its independence, but it became particularly frosty after an incident in 1807 in which the warship HMS *Leopard* ordered the United States frigate *Chesepeake* to stop so it could be searched for deserters from the Royal Navy, then opened fire when the *Chesepeake*'s captain refused. War was only narrowly averted. Animosity between the two nations only grew more intense over the next five years, with many people in the U.S. calling for a declaration of war and an invasion of their northern neighbours, the British colonies of Upper and Lower Canada.

By 1812, President James Madison and the "War Hawks" in Congress thought the timing for war was finally right. Napoleon Bonaparte's France was at the height of its power, and Britain stood virtually alone in Europe against this enemy; only Sicily, Sardinia, Sweden and Portugal were outside France's influence. It took all of Britain's resources to oppose Napoleon and stave off defeat in its war with France that had been going on for more than a decade, so there would be little help available for the defence of Canada should America invade. In addition, Madison's government convinced itself, erroneously as it turned out, that most of Canada's French-speaking population would welcome liberation from Britain. Even the English-speaking population of Canada was deemed of dubious loyalty to the Crown; as many as one-third had come from the U.S. less than a generation ago.

There's no doubt that the odds seemed favourable for an easy American victory: the population of the United States in 1812 numbered just over seven million people, compared with 500,000 people living in all of Canada. However, Madison over-estimated popular support for the war. Many people in New York and Vermont profited greatly by trading with Canada, and with war this trade would be lost. There was also little fervor for war in the southern states. Madison also failed to appreciate the strength of Britain, even when engaged in a life-and-death battle with France: her army was battle hardened and led by excellent officers, her navy was by far the largest in the world, her industrial strength exceeded that of America by a very wide margin and, home to 12.5 million people, she had almost double the population. Nevertheless, President Madison was set on war.

1812

On June 1, 1812, President James Madison asked Congress to declare war. The reasons he and his supporters listed were less substantive than emotional in nature. The British policy of interdicting all neutral maritime trade with Napoleon Bonaparte's France led to the seizure of numerous American merchant ships, causing anger and some financial distress to American business. Even more offensive to American pride was the Royal Navy's practice of impressing into their service American merchant crewmen who could not prove they were not

British subjects (a result of the frequency in which British sailors escaped service in the Royal Navy by enlisting aboard American ships). At the same time, there were widespread but largely baseless rumours that the British were encouraging Indian attacks on American frontier settlements. Diplomatic efforts to defuse the growing crisis came too late. On June 18, the American government found itself swept up by national war fever that was at a boiling point. With votes of 79 to 49 in the House of Representatives and 19 to 13 in the Senate, the United States declared war on Britain. Their aim was invade and conquer Canada, which many Americans believed would eagerly embrace American republicanism.

The Americans envisioned a three-pronged simultaneous invasion of Canada across the Detroit, Niagara and St. Lawrence rivers. It was an ambitious plan intended to divide and overwhelm the vastly outnumbered defenders. Unfortunately, the small and ill-prepared U.S. Army, led by over-the-hill political appointees, was unprepared for war and failed to live up to the task. Instead, invasion became piecemeal over several months. By mid-August the westernmost of these attacks had been utterly defeated, with the losses of Fort Mackinac (July 17), Fort Dearborn (August 15) and Detroit (August 16) leaving most of the Northwest Territory (comprising modern Ohio, Michigan, Indiana and adjoining regions) under British control. The central attack, across the Niagara frontier, floundered in October with a humiliating defeat at Queenston Heights (October 13), the battle that saw the death of British General Isaac Brock and his birth as a Canadian hero. The easternmost attack accomplished little as well, petering out by the end of November after two half-hearted attempts against Montreal that met stiff resistance from defending forces.

The United States had lost every battle of significance, had suffered losses in prestige, men and supplies, and had even lost territory to the British. The ramifications of the string of military failures in 1812 shook the American political administration. President Madison held onto his office in the fall elections, but he was forced to replace his Secretary of War. But despite being humbled, the Americans were not about to concede defeat. They would spend the winter redoubling their efforts in preparation for renewed fighting in 1813.

On the other side of the border, the mood by year's end was buoyant. Despite the sobering loss of General Brock, there was much to celebrate in Canada. The country had been forced into a war for which it was unprepared and undersupplied, and yet it had defeated the Americans at every turn. Problems remained, however, as it was recognized that the war was only just beginning and was likely to be a long one, with new and additional sacrifices to come.

1813

Throughout 1813 the Americans continued to try to press their attacks on Canada. They captured Fort George at the mouth of the Niagara River (May 27) but suffered defeat in bloody battles—Stoney Creek (June 6), Forty

Mile Creek (June 7) and Beaver Dams (June 24)—whenever they tried to advance inland. The campaign fought on the Niagara frontier ended in stalemate, but there in particular the war took on an increasingly brutal tenor. In December the Americans burned a number of villages, including St. Davids and Niagara (modern-day Niagara-on-the-Lake), where they threw the populace out into the snow. This cruelty enraged the British-Canadian forces and led to reprisals against Buffalo and other communities along the Niagara River, which were similarly burned. Areas along the Niagara frontier were rapidly becoming a barren wasteland of scorched villages, abandoned farms and terrified, hungry families.

Farther to the west, American fortunes were far better. On Lake Erie an American fleet led by Commodore Oliver Hazard Perry decisively defeated a British squadron led by Commodore H.R. Barclay on September 10. Perry's victory made the strategic British positions on the western end of the lake—Fort Malden and Detroit—suddenly very vulnerable. Outnumbered and under pressure from an advancing American army led by Brigadier General William Harrison, the British abandoned both of these isolated positions and fell back into the interior of Upper Canada. The Americans followed. On October 5, Harrison caught up with the retreating British army at the Thames River and destroyed it in a bloody day of battle. As a result, most of southwestern Upper Canada fell under American military control.

The loss of Lake Erie and much of southern Ontario also threatened to cut off British positions even farther west, including the strategic Fort Mackinac on Lake

Huron. While the fort, under siege and with diminishing supplies, managed to hold on, most of the Northwest Territory fell.

The year 1813 also saw a two-pronged American attack toward Montreal, which was intended to sever the St. Lawrence River and thereby isolate Upper Canada. This invasion ended in inglorious defeat; one prong, consisting of some 3000 men, was defeated by a force one-third its size at the Battle of Crysler's Farm (November 11) along the banks of the St. Lawrence, while the second wing of similar size suffered humiliating defeat at the hands of a mere 300 defenders at Chateauguay (October 26). What was notable about these British victories is that they were won largely by Franco-Canadian forces, giving proof to the lie that the populace of Lower Canada (Quebec) was treasonous and merely awaiting the right moment to throw off the British yoke.

Despite these defeats, the United States emerged from the second year of the war in a better position than they had in 1812. With a number of victories behind them, they had regained most of the territory lost the previous year in the west and occupied a small part of southwestern Upper Canada. The third year of fighting promised to be decisive. Would the heavily outnumbered British, Canadians and First Nations continue to hold their own, or would American strength finally wear down the opposition?

By the end of 1813, the immediate threat had once again been thwarted, thanks to the British military victories at Chateauguay, Crysler's Farm and Fort Niagara. Despite these successes, the military situation for the continued defence of Upper Canada was not a positive one. Battlefield losses and the extensive territory they were expected to defend necessitated not only replacement troops but also substantial reinforcements if they were to maintain their temporary advantage, to say nothing of recovering the territory lost in southwestern Ontario. Unfortunately, few troops were on their way to Upper Canada, causing British generals there to anticipate the 1814 campaigning season with trepidation.

The war was just as back and forth at sea as it was on land. The Royal Navy, the largest fleet in the world by far, quickly neutralized the small U.S. Navy. To compensate, the United States began licensing privateers to seize enemy merchant ships for profit in a kind of legalized piracy. By early 1813, some 600 American privateers, mostly from the New England states, were scourging British commerce in the Atlantic, the Caribbean, the North Sea and even the English Channel. By the end of the year they had taken over 1300 British merchant ships. And yet, while undoubtedly a nuisance, the impact of privateers on the war effort was minor. Value of British trade actually grew dramatically over the course of the war, making it apparent that privateers were not doing much to degrade Britain's ability to wage war.

The event that had the greatest impact on the ocean war was the Royal Navy's blockade on the American coast, which began modestly in 1812 but by 1813 covered much of the Atlantic coast and began to strangle American trade. Between 1811 and 1814, the value of American exports and imports fell from $114 million to $20 million and the customs revenues needed to finance the war fell from $13 million to $6 million. The United States clearly needed to end the war quickly, before it went bankrupt. By necessity, 1814 would have to be a decisive year for the war. Either the United States would have to conquer Canada outright or begin the process of negotiating a settlement.

1814

Across the Atlantic in Europe, the military events of 1813 had improved Britain's position and presented the possibility that far more resources could be applied to the American war in 1814 than had previously been available. The defeat of Britain's continental enemy, Napoleon Bonaparte's France, meant significant numbers of reinforcements could be sent to Canada. The Americans knew they had to take advantage of the few months that lay ahead before these fresh British troops arrived. Consequently, that spring the Americans renewed their attack on the Niagara frontier. On July 3, a well-trained, 3500-strong American force captured Fort Erie at the mouth of the Niagara River, and then, on July 5, soundly defeated a British army led by General Phineas Riall at the Battle of Chippawa. A few weeks later the armies clashed again at the Battle of Lundy's Lane (July 25). This was the bloodiest battle in the war to date, and the most confusing, as it raged well into the night. As daylight returned, the intensity of the night's carnage became all too clear. The battlefield was covered with lines of bodies, marking where the opposing regiments had stood, fought and died, sometimes within feet of each other.

Although the Battle of Lundy's Lane was indecisive, it weakened the Americans so badly that they could not continue their offensive and retired to the defences of Fort Erie. In the following weeks British reinforcements began to arrive, and they launched a costly, ill-planned and ultimately unsuccessful assault against the fort (August 15). Nevertheless, despite this bloody failure, the British had, by November, driven the Americans out of the Niagara Peninsula entirely.

To the east, the situation was reversed. Here the British, under General Sir George Prevost, had launched an invasion of their own, with 12,000 men marching down the shores of Lake Champlain toward Albany, New York. Sailing alongside was a naval squadron of four ships and 12 galleys that provided vital transport support. At Plattsburgh (September 11), this British fleet was intercepted by a squadron under American Commodore Thomas Macdonough. The battle was a decisive victory for the Americans; not a single British vessel escaped. Deprived of the naval support necessary for supplying his troops, Prevost concluded that his invasion could not succeed and decided to return to Canada.

In the meantime, British naval landings along the American eastern seaboard captured or sacked numerous villages and towns. The most significant amphibious landings took place in August and September. A British force sailed into Chesapeake Bay and landed a sizable army that marched on a virtually undefended Washington, D.C. After brushing aside an American force at the Battle of Bladensburg (August 24), the British captured the capital and, in retaliation for the American razing of York (modern-day Toronto), burned all prominent government buildings including the White House and the Capitol. This force then re-embarked and sailed to Baltimore. There, they ran into an extensive series of earthworks that had been thrown up by the Maryland militia and a spirited defence that halted the land assault. Meanwhile, Vice-Admiral Alexander Cochrane's powerful naval squadron could not force its way past Fort McHenry at the entrance to Baltimore's harbour, nor did it succeed in shelling the fortress into submission (September 13–14). As a result, the attack was called off and Baltimore was saved from Washington's fiery fate.

Frustrated at Baltimore, the British force returned to the West Indies and began planning an attack on New Orleans. For this new operation the British assembled 8000 veteran troops under the command of Major General Sir Edward Pakenham, and some 50 supporting warships and transports. Defending the city were 5700 troops, mostly militia and volunteers, under the command of future president Major General Andrew Jackson. The British came on shore on December 23 and marched toward New Orleans. Protecting the city lay high earthwork fortifications well defended by artillery. When the British attempted a frontal assault on January 8, 1815, the inevitable result was carnage—2000 British dead, among them Pakenham. The shattered British expeditionary force withdrew to the coast, where they learned that peace negotiations had been concluded in Ghent two weeks earlier.

Aftermath

The War of 1812 had been an almost pointless war. During negotiations, the Americans realized they held a poor hand. Far from conquering Canada, they had actually lost more territory to Britain than they had gained. Much of Maine had been lost to the British, as had vast swaths of Michigan Territory, Illinois Territory (modern-day Wisconsin) and northern Indiana Territory. To make matters worse, the war had become so unpopular that some states threatened to secede from the Union in protest. The best the United States could hope for was status quo. Thankfully for them, the British public was exhausted by two decades of war—first against Napoleon's France, and then against the U.S.—and were clamoring for peace. As a consequence, British negotiators were happy for any speedy resolution to the fighting and agreed to return to pre-war borders. A treaty, signed in the Belgian city of Ghent on Christmas Eve, 1814, put an official end to the fighting. After three years of war and thousands of lives lost, nothing had been gained by either side, save perhaps for a heightened sense of nationalism.

That being said, most historians agree that the War of 1812 represented a British victory. Britain succeeded in defending its North American colonies, ensuring Canada would remain separate from the United States and eventually become an independent country. This was the most significant outcome of the conflict. For Britain, the retention of these colonies gave it access to North American products outside of the control of the United States, and also contributed to the overall strength of the Empire.

One shudders to think how Britain would have fared in both 1914 and 1939 without the absolutely critical support Canada provided (while the United States kept out of World Wars I and II until 1917 and 1941, respectively).

It's important to remember the War of 1812 and the sacrifices of the fallen soldiers on both sides. It's also important to remember that, other than a few squabbles here and there, Canada and the United States have been allies, and great friends, for two centuries and counting. That perhaps is the enduring legacy of the War of 1812.

Battle of Queenston Heights

Queenston Heights must surely be Canada's most poignant battle site. A huge stone monument towers, sentry-like, over the site where hundreds of men died and serves to commemorate the burial place of Canada's saviour, General Sir Isaac Brock, who fell at the head of his troops. Anyone who steps foot within the park instantly recognizes this as hallowed ground, a place where soldiers were shot down and a young nation was born. The raw emotion of the battle, the death of a beloved general and the appalling suffering of the wounded and dying have all left their mark on Queenston Heights, and ghosts from that long-ago conflict abound at what is today a National Historic Site.

General Isaac Brock's eternal path is the road leading to Queenston Heights.

How many ghosts are there? If, as many people believe, ghosts are born of the trauma of life's last moments, then entire companies of ghosts might exist on this former battleground. After all, young men had their futures ripped away from them in the most traumatic way imaginable. Certainly the Battle of Queenston Heights does not rest comfortably within the confines of history books. Not only has the brutal fighting of that day left a solemn impression that can still be felt on the battlefield today, but also, many people insist that the 200-year-old battle occasionally erupts from the past to be re-fought by spectral soldiers in the land of the living.

The spectral fighting witnessed by visitors at Queenston Heights is an echo of that which took place during the tumultuous first year of the War of 1812. It seems the ghosts of those soldiers who died during the battle want us to remember their sacrifice. Sadly, few in Canada know much about the circumstances surrounding this bitter fight and why the area is haunted by countless spirits to this day.

In June of 1812, the United States declared war on Britain and laid plans to attack across the Niagara River to cut Upper Canada in half and demoralize the enemy, rendering the country indefensible by British forces. The offensive began on October 12 when artillery batteries along the entire length of the river opened fire in an attempt to confuse the British regarding the actual location of the crossing. Around 3:00 AM on October 13, 600 American troops piled into rowboats and pulled out into the river, headed for the small Canadian village of Queenston and the strategic heights that loomed above it.

Queenston Heights dominates the entire region. Part of the Niagara Escarpment, it's a huge rocky ridge rising 100 metres above the river, affording anyone who possessed it unmatched observation of the surrounding area and superior artillery positions. The British recognized the importance of Queenston Heights and had built a fortification atop it, housing an 18-pound cannon that commanded the river.

As the American boats approached shore in a cold drizzle, they were greeted by artillery and musket fire. Although the invaders suffered heavily, they persevered and eventually reached the Canadian side of the river, splashing ashore amidst a hail of bullets and with driving rain pelting their faces. But there they stalled, the withering artillery and musketry preventing any progress. It looked for a time as if the Americans would be wiped out on the riverbank, but a small patrol suddenly changed the complexion of the battle. While most of the invaders were hemmed in along the river's edge, a party of 60 men led by Captain John E. Wool found a treacherously steep path that led to the heights. They managed to climb up, pulling themselves by root and rock, and surprised the defenders. With the heights and the deadly 18-pound gun in American hands, the tide of battle swung and now the invaders had the upper hand. Soon, hundreds of American soldiers had assembled on the easily defensible Queenston Heights.

Meanwhile, eight miles away at Fort George, Major General Isaac Brock, commander of British troops in Upper Canada, rounded up about 200 reinforcements and rushed to the battlefield. Brock led a desperate counter-attack to retake the heights. The general, leading his troops, sword flashing, was clearly visible to the enemy. His bravery was a magnificent sight and an inspiration to his men, but Brock was also an easy target for enemy shooters. Without warning, an American rifleman emerged from the brush, took careful aim and fired at the general. Brock was hit in the chest and stumbled, clutching desperately at the wound. He was dead within moments but the battle raged on, filling the air with the noise of cannon balls and bullets, the clang of swords and the moans of the wounded and dying.

Brock's successor, Major General Roger Hale Sheaffe, ordered more troops and allied Native warriors to converge on Queenston. The warriors were the first on the scene. They ascended the heights inland, out of range and sight of the Americans, and then began sniping at the enemy from the cover of the dense forest. Whooping loudly, they would charge forward and then melt back into the forest like ghosts, their war cries echoing through the woods and unnerving the American soldiers.

Meanwhile, Sheaffe had assembled 900 men and led them up a steep path onto the heights. After ordering a single volley fired at the shaken Americans, the British soldiers charged with bayonets fixed. They needed no encouragement. To a man they wanted vengeance for the loss of the beloved General Brock. The assault was so determined, so overwhelming in its ferocity that it took less than 15 minutes for the American resistance to collapse. Many American soldiers died by bullet or bayonet. Some fell from the cliff in a desperate bid for escape and were dashed on the rocks below. A few did manage to get back to the boats. But most of them simply threw down their weapons in surrender. The battle that had started around 3:00 AM that morning ended around 3:00 PM. During 12 hours of fighting, the Americans lost as many as 250 men, most buried where they fell, their graves unmarked and forgotten.

Memories of that bloody, corpse-strewn battlefield took years to fade, but they didn't disappear entirely. The raw emotion of the battle, the death of a beloved general and the appalling suffering of so many people have all left their mark on the land. Queenston Heights is a picturesque parkland today, but its beauty masks wounds that are not yet fully healed.

Ghosts from that long-ago conflict abound on the towering heights. These spirits—individually and in company strength—have been appearing for as far back as anyone can remember. It's said that phantom sounds of battle carry upon the breeze: the pitiful moans of wounded and dying men and animals; the roar of cannons; the echo of musketry; the harsh bark of commands; spine-chilling Indian war cries; and the marching of hundreds of invisible boots in practiced unison. Other people feel the heavy loss of life weighing down on them, darkening their mood and bringing them to the point of tears. Sometimes, this unsettling sensation is accompanied by a stench in the air, a nauseating blend of gunpowder and blood.

Lengthy and mysterious cold spots are felt. It might be that these mark the lines along which the opposing armies stood and faced one another, and where men dropped and died when a bullet struck home. Or perhaps they mark trench-graves where the American dead were hastily interred after the battle.

The restaurant atop the heights is a popular dining place, famed for good food and warm hospitality. However, employees claim there's a side to the building unknown to the public, that of uncanny sounds without obvious source and a tradition of being inexplicably "creepy" after midnight. The location of the artillery redan is similarly heavily haunted.

It isn't just sounds and sensations that people experience at Queenston Heights. Sometimes the encounter is visual in nature, involving sights that leave the witness' heart frozen somewhere between fear and awe. Some say if you look closely when day gives way to darkness, ghostly soldiers can be seen rising up from the earth and wandering the former battleground. Other reports suggest that the time of day has little bearing on one's chances of having an otherworldly encounter, that apparitions have been seen during full daylight marching through the parkland, completely oblivious to the living.

One individual, walking his dog through the lightly wooded grounds one morning, unwittingly stumbled into an otherworldly battle. A gentle breeze passing through the trees created a soothing rustle as the leaves stirred, hinting at a beautiful day to come. Suddenly the wind began to gust, bending trees and whipping foliage into a frenzy. Moments later, the man saw the bright flare of muskets lighting up the murky dawn, and in the momentary orange flashes he could make out the grim faces of soldiers in the midst of a life-or-death struggle. The anxious barking of his dog merged with the sounds of cannons thundering in the distance and, nearer, rifles being fired. Perhaps half a minute later the din of combat died.

It didn't tail off, as one would expect, with the occasional discharge of a weapon or the pained moans of the wounded, but rather ended instantly and completely, leaving a deathly silence in its wake. Even the wind had returned to its previous gentle caress. It was as if the entire event hadn't even occurred.

Sometimes the ghostly soldiers spill off the battlefield and over the sides of the escarpment to intrude upon the surrounding lands. Apparitions of American soldiers disembarking from boats have been reported down near the shoreline. They clamber out of their rowboats and race for cover, ducking as if to avoid ethereal bullets fired by unseen British defenders. One particularly fantastic report had a line of soldiers emerging from below the waters of the Niagara River, rising up from the deep to march inland. At first glance this tale sounds too far-fetched to be true, but deeper examination leads one to wonder. It turns out that owing to the damming of the river upstream, the Niagara has actually risen many feet since the War of 1812. Therefore, the points at which the invaders came ashore during the Battle of Queenston Heights would indeed be submerged today.

In 2006, during an early evening like any other, a young man was driving along York Road as it skirts the heights. The sun had set and shadows were stretching across the landscape, but he found himself enjoying the scenery and was in no particular hurry. He slowed the car to admire the many historical homes along the road and to marvel at the picturesque Niagara Escarpment. This young native of Niagara was familiar with the blood-soaked history of the region and even its long tradition of hauntings, but in all the times he had driven this stretch of road not a single thing had occurred to make him believe restless souls walked alongside the area's countless tourists. He simply didn't believe in ghosts. His views changed forever that evening.

He slowed the car to a crawl as he approached a small, unassuming stone monument standing alongside the road. He had never seen this marker before, or certainly had not taken notice of it. Curious as to its significance, he pulled to the side of the road and had his hand on the car door to climb out when suddenly he saw at least a dozen red-coated soldiers marching in single file across the road only a few feet in front of him. The young man couldn't believe his eyes; he could almost see through the soldiers, whose skin, uniforms and equipment were all luminescent, the colour of moonlight. He watched as they passed by the stone monument and began marching up the side of the escarpment with muskets at the ready for battle. The vision lasted only a few seconds before the soldiers slowly faded from view as the woods swallowed them up. The witness could hardly believe his eyes, and it was long moments before his racing heart slowed to a more rhythmic beat.

When finally he had the courage to exit his vehicle, he approached the stone marker on unsteady legs. He learned that the modest monument commemorates the location where the British army, under the command of General Roger Hale Sheaffe, climbed the cliff to attack the American army and thus win the Battle of Queenston Heights. Had this young man witnessed the echo of a moment in time from almost two centuries ago? Were the spirits he saw those of Sheaffe's command who fell in his victorious counter-attack? It certainly seemed so.

The most famous spectre associated with the Battle of Queenston Heights is that of the battle's most famous participant: General Isaac Brock. Perhaps as befitting a man of his legendary stature, Brock's apparition is noted in several locations throughout Niagara. A Canadian hero, the man credited with saving Canada from American occupation, Brock deserves no less.

To this day, a Union Jack flies over the spot at which the general is believed to have died. Here, some people report feeling overwhelming sadness and despair that brings them to the verge of tears. One person is said to have heard a disembodied voice cry out, "Onward!" He believed it to be Brock urging his soldiers forward when they began to falter after he was fatally wounded. It may have been Brock encouraging his troops, but it almost certainly wasn't an echo of words he spoke upon being wounded; the general was shot in the lung, and excruciating pain combined with blood pouring into that lung would have made it almost impossible for him to speak in the moments he had before death claimed him.

Atop Queenston Heights stands the imposing, inspiring and hauntingly beautiful Brock's Monument, towering 185 feet above the contested field over which British and American soldiers fought. The main entrance is flanked by two large mulberry trees believed to have been planted during the 1850s. Upon entering, you find brass plaques to Brock and Lieutenant Colonel John Macdonell (also killed in the battle), and another in tribute to the British, Canadian and First Nations soldiers who died at the Battle of Queenston Heights. The bodies of the two fallen officers are interred in crypts within the limestone walls. There are also educational displays outlining Brock's life, the battle and the monument's history. A 235-step spiral staircase up the column leads visitors to a small platform underneath Brock's statue, affording spectacular views over the surrounding Niagara region and Lake Ontario—the land Brock died to keep out of American hands. The monument is somber at the best of times, but some say there are times it becomes actually spooky. Inside, one may hear weird and potentially psychic knocks, groans and whispers.

Brock's Monument is a reminder of the suffering and sacrifice that took place 200 years ago.

Other places where Brock's proud, imposing ghost is reputed to make unexpected appearances are a private home in Queenston, which was built upon the foundation of a tavern where the general's body was taken immediately after he was killed; the northeast bastion at Fort George (also known as the Cavalier Bastion or the York Battery), where he and Colonel Macdonell were initially buried; and even his ancestral home in Guernsey, Brock House, suggesting his spirit occasionally returns home even if his physical body remains in Canada.

Brock's most famous apparition, however, takes the form of a phantom galloping hell-bent along the road from Niagara-on-the-Lake to Queenston Heights. It seems the tragic general is doomed to forever re-enact a ride that culminated in his untimely death. Legend goes that General Brock was awakened before dawn on October 13, 1812, by the sounds of weapons firing from Queenston. This is most unlikely, since the storm that night would have drowned out the noise of battle at such a distance. It's more likely that a dispatch rider arrived at his quarters with news of the American landing. Brock hurriedly dressed, then raced out into the still-dark early morning. He knew speed was of the essence. It was an eight-mile ride to Queenston along a country lane crossing many ravines and marshy creeks. If he was to play a role in the unfolding battle, he knew he had leave immediately and ride as fast as his mount could carry him. Without waiting for any attendants to join him, he put his spurs to his horse and galloped into the darkness. Brock arrived at Queenston around 5:00 AM, began organizing the defenders and then led a counter-attack up to the now American-held heights that ended in failure when he was shot down.

Ever since that fateful day, locals have spoken of a spectral horseman seen racing down the Niagara Parkway (which in most places follows the route of the old 1812-era road), and many of them believe this to be General Brock's proud shade riding to battle. Those who see him say that he is a tall, powerfully built man with handsome features wearing a red British uniform. It certainly sounds like Brock. Sometimes people hear and feel the ghost rather than see him, the thundering of horse's hooves accompanied by an uncomfortable chill letting them know the desperate general has just passed by.

General and private alike, the soldiers who fought and died for Queenston Heights are tortured in the afterlife. Despite their bravery, service and sacrifice, the battle continues to haunt the souls of those who fell that October day. It seems tragic that the horrors of war should endure beyond the grave. Once the dead have been laid to rest, shouldn't the rattle of muskets and the roar of cannons finally recede to allow for a peaceful final sleep? One would like to think so, and yet Queenston Heights—like countless battlefields around the world—shows that the psychological scars of war linger well after the physical ones have healed. And so we have to ask ourselves, will these restless spirits that continue to wage their phantom battle ever agree to a truce and put an end to 200 years of fighting? Or are they to continue killing and dying for this strategic position, locked forever in a battle with no end? Time will only tell.

Ghost Ships: *Hamilton* and *Scourge*

The Great Lakes swallow ships and souls by the thousand. Dangerous shoals lurking unseen beneath the waves, terrible storms that strike up without notice and rage mercilessly against vessels unlucky enough to be in their paths, and cold waves that churn the water's surface are but a few of the terrors awaiting those who sail the five expansive lakes. In days of old, every veteran mariner who sailed the Great Lakes could tell enough tales of death and danger to fill every night of a month-long voyage. The most terrifying were those of ghost ships. The Great Lakes are prowled by a number of vessels with no man at their helm, each one the result of a terrible tragedy that saw passengers and crew dragged to the bottom of the lake along with the stricken vessel. Mariners were so superstitious that the mere whisper of a ghost ship could cause even the bravest man's courage to fail him.

Sightings of lone ghost ships, if these old maritime tales are to be believed, were relatively commonplace. Far rarer were stories involving more than one ghostly vessel. Rare, but not unheard of, because ever since the War of 1812 a pair of spectral warships, the USS *Hamilton* and the USS *Scourge*, have been seen sailing upon the waters of Lake Ontario by startled witnesses. Trapped aboard their rotting hulls are the phantoms of almost 50 sailors for whom their ships are a watery prison that prevents them from moving on and finding lasting peace.

Beware if you see two ghost ships like this one while sailing Lake Ontario.

The *Hamilton* and the *Scourge* didn't start their careers as warships, but as commercial vessels designed to transport goods rather than soldiers and cannons. Originally called the *Diana*, the *Hamilton* was built in Oswego, New York, in 1809 for merchant Matthew McNair. She spent a few years plying Lake Ontario before the War of 1812 erupted and she was purchased by the U.S. Navy, which renamed her *Hamilton* in honour of the Secretary of the Navy, Paul Hamilton.

The *Scourge* was built for James Crooks, a merchant living in Niagara (now Niagara-on-the-Lake), and was originally called *Lord Nelson* after Admiral Horatio Nelson, the British naval hero who won the Battle of Trafalgar. On June 9, 1812—just nine days before war was declared—she was travelling on Lake Ontario when she was stopped by the American warship *Oneida* and impounded on the suspicion of smuggling. There was never any thought of returning the vessel to its rightful owner. As soon as war broke out she was handed over to the U.S. Navy, refitted into a warship and renamed *Scourge*.

Neither vessel was ideally suited to its new role. They were small, shallow draft vessels so that the addition of cannons on the top decks made them top-heavy and liable to rolling in rough weather. This characteristic was to have tragic repercussions.

By the summer of 1813, both ships were part of a squadron commanded by Commodore Isaac Chauncey. In early August, Chauncey attacked the British at York (now Toronto). The Americans defeated the small garrison, captured the town and burned the public buildings. With smoke rising from the ravaged community, Chauncey withdrew his fleet to the Niagara River. There, on the morning of August 7, the American ships were spotted by a British fleet commanded by Commodore James Yeo. Battle was inevitable. As soon as the Americans realized they had been seen their ships got underway, firing a broadside at the enemy as they slowly sailed out of the river and onto the expanse of Lake Ontario. The lack of wind kept the combatants from getting close enough to do real damage, so throughout the day the enemies only managed to exchange occasional shots at one another.

Toward evening the wind, barely a breeze to begin with, died off completely and turned the lake as smooth as a sheet of glass. All of the vessels in both squadrons were becalmed, unable to move. The fleets were within sight of one another but too far away for any fighting. Canvas hung limp from their masts. The fighting would have to wait until the rise of the sun the following morning. Aboard the *Scourge* and the *Hamilton*, sailors quickly fell asleep. Gunners dozed at their stations in case the wind suddenly picked up and fighting resumed; most of the others slept on deck. Some may have noticed that the stars were blotted out by gathering clouds above, but certainly no one aboard either vessel had any idea what lay in store that night.

Sometime after midnight rain began to fall. At first it was a light drizzle, but it rapidly escalated into a violent storm that saw the rain driving down with relentless fury and the lake grow suddenly vicious. The wind gained in velocity with each passing moment. A violent squall that appeared seemingly out of nowhere roared down on the ships sitting at anchor. The lake was transformed into heaving mountains that rushed out of the dark and pounded the ships. Thunder rumbled ominously overhead, lightning crashed like a hundred cannons firing at once, and the howling wind filled the ships' sails and tossed them about like toys. Sailors grabbed hold of anything that was battened down to prevent themselves from being thrown about the bucking ships. Unable to fight the tempest, the unfortunate crews could only stare into the face of death as they waited in terror for the ships to take their final plunge into the restless depths. Some men fell to their knees and begged the heavens for salvation, but most simply resigned themselves to their fate.

The end they dreaded wasn't long in coming. Massive waves crashed relentlessly against the ships' hulls, causing water to rush onto their decks and filling their holds. Suddenly there was a mournful groan, and then the two top-heavy ships simply rolled over and sank to the bottom of the lake. It had all happened so fast that only a few sailors were able to dive overboard before the ships went down. These lucky few struggled to stay afloat in the violent waters. They heard the pathetic cries of those trapped aboard as the ships filled with water and slipped from sight but could do nothing but mourn the bitter deaths of their friends and fellow crewmen. Most of two ships' crews, 53 men out of a total of 72, were trapped aboard and drowned as the two vessels settled on the lake bed. The *Hamilton* and the *Scourge* became their watery caskets, a mass aquatic grave.

Perhaps worse than being denied a proper burial was the fact that these sailors, and the wrecks on which they were imprisoned, were quickly forgotten. They became little more than a footnote in a war few people had any real interest in remembering. For well over a century no one even knew exactly where the ships went down. That changed in 1975 when Daniel A. Nelson, an amateur marine archeologist, found both the *Hamilton* and the *Scourge*. They lay 300 feet below the surface of the lake, both sitting upright on the bottom, remarkably well preserved by the frigid water of Lake Ontario. Both vessels were eerily intact, still-solid wooden prisons entombing the dead.

But while their physical rest may have been undisturbed over the past two centuries, the same cannot be said of the spirits of those who died aboard these ships. It wasn't long after they went down that old salts on the lake began to whisper to one another about a pair of spectral vessels prowling about like menacing predators. These small, square-rigged craft would be seen stalking another ship through the depths of a bank of fog, or looming through the drenching rain of a thunder storm. Some rare sightings even occurred on clear days, and were real enough that witnesses were overcome with genuine fear as they watched sailors on the ships' decks preparing to fire cannons at them. The skipper of the targeted vessel would order full-steam or additional sails sent aloft as he desperately spun the wheel to flee from the scene, all the while expecting screaming cannon balls to begin splintering his ship at any moment.

These sightings continued well into the 20th century. More than one crew of a freighter plying Lake Ontario was startled to see two small sailing vessels riding on, or just above, the waves. It would have been immediately clear that these ships were not of the present time, their rigging and design all wrong for a recreational sailing boat. One report added a few new sinister wrinkles to the age-old tale. In that version, a strange yellow glow was seen radiating through the open gun ports of the hulls of both the *Hamilton* and the *Scourge*. Seconds later, the ships vibrated violently before listing to one side and sliding below the waves, leaving only the shrieking of drowning sailors. These cries lasted for only a few moments before they were silenced as the spirits of the dead followed their ships below the waves. As suddenly as the ghost ships had come, they were gone.

Sighting any ghost ship is considered an ill omen, but if maritime lore is to be believed, sighting two wrecks

crewed by undead sailors has particularly dire consequences. Should a ship encounter the *Scourge* and the
Hamilton, misfortune was sure to follow soon after. It was
even worse if these spectral vessels crossed your wake: in
such circumstances one of your crew would surely die.

This superstition isn't merely from a more innocent
era, either. As late as 1942, several crewmen aboard the
steamer *Cayuga* claimed to have seen the *Scourge* and
the *Hamilton* cut the wake of their ship just before sunset
one day. As if the sight of two ethereal warships faintly
glowing in the gathering dusk wasn't enough cause for
alarm, the crewmen noticed with concern the panicked
reaction of the ship's steward. A weathered old sailor who
had stared into the face of the angriest storms and never
showed the slightest sign of fear, after sighting the ghost
ships his hands began to shake uncontrollably and his
eyes took on the look of a cornered wild animal.

The concerned *Cayuga* crew asked the steward what
he was so afraid of. In a raspy voice, pipe clamped tightly
between yellowed teeth, the old man informed them of
the legend of the *Scourge* and the *Hamilton*, and the dire
repercussions of seeing them. "Death will come aboard
this boat soon enough," he assured them solemnly. The
crewmen grew fearful. Who would the curse claim?
The answer came with the rising of the sun the following
morning when the old steward was found lifeless in his
bunk, eyes staring unfocused at the ceiling above.

Perhaps the most terrifying encounter with the two
warships is also among the most recent, dating back to
around the time the lost wrecks were discovered by
Daniel Nelson. Mark Ranson was a lifelong recreational

sailor who had guided his sailboat from one end of Lake Ontario and back again numerous times, and while he had a healthy respect for the power of the lake, he had never once encountered anything that truly caused him terror. That changed during a fateful trip from Toronto to Niagara-on-the-Lake. It was late in the afternoon on a pleasant midsummer day. A warm, blustery wind had carried his boat at a brisk pace across the lake, and Mark found himself with little to do but enjoy the sun on his skin and the view out across the placid lake.

Suddenly, the wind died. One minute the sails had been full, the next they hung limply against the mast. It was eerily calm and an unsettling silence settled over the lake. The only sound was the screeching of gulls that inexplicably fled in panicked flight, and when they disappeared there was nothing to break the unnatural quiet. Clouds, heavy and grey, appeared in the sky and crowded out the sun. Then a dark fog settled over the water.

Mark had never seen such a dramatic turn of weather before in all his decades of sailing. There was no rational reason to be alarmed, and yet he found himself unsettled and feeling trapped aboard his boat. Without warning, two dark shapes loomed out of the thick fog ahead. They were 19th-century sailing ships, lit in a peculiar shade of yellow, cannons lining their decks. No one manned the ships' helms, and their rigging swayed directionless on rotted masts. Mark watched as the listless phantom ships slowly glided past. Then they seemed to be effortlessly tossed about by an unseen force and, seconds later, sank beneath the waves, leaving only the cries of drowning sailors behind.

Moments later, the fog began to dissipate, the clouds above parted to once again reveal the summer sun, and a gentle breeze filled his boat's sails. It was as if nothing unusual had happened. But Mark knew different. His body still shook with the fright, and he wanted nothing more than to get off the lake as fast as humanly possible, to stand on dry land where he knew he would be safe from the haunts lurking beneath the waters of Lake Ontario.

The wrecks of the USS *Hamilton* and the USS *Scourge* rest on the bottom of Lake Ontario, remaining undisturbed despite their discovery. They are silent and poignant evidence of one night of terror in a long-ago war, and they are the solemn graves of more than 50 souls. But the two old fighting ships and their crew do not rest peacefully. On occasion, unknown forces raise them from the depths to prowl the waves of Lake Ontario. The dark holds of these creaking, ghostly vessels are home to restless spirits and nameless terrors. Death and misfortune follow in their wake. Do the dead sailors bear a hunger for men's souls?

Captain Swayze and the Olde Angel Inn

Colin Swayze does his best not to worry, but his heart is heavy and he is deathly afraid. Another hour has gone by and still his beloved, Euretta, has not stolen away from her watchful father to join him. How many nights has it been since she's met him in the basement of the inn for their secret rendezvous? As midnight approaches there is still no sign of her, but the young man waits optimistically, certain she will arrive soon. But as the hours pass, a dreadful fear grows in the pit of his stomach. He grows restless and begins pacing the wooden floors. His previous caution disappears and he begins to wander about the building, searching desperately for Euretta. *We promised never to be apart from one another, so where can she be*, he wonders to himself.

It's a question Captain Colin Swayze has been asking nightly for 200 years as he maintains a lonely vigil for his betrothed. He waits patiently for her to join him in Niagara's Olde Angel Inn, unaware that his time to leave is long past. Tragically, he has not realized that as long as he remains earthbound he can never be reunited with her. Nor does he seem to realize that it was his premature and tragic death that separated him from her. But for one ill-conceived decision born of passion, the two might have enjoyed a long and happy life together.

The Olde Angel Inn is an English-style pub located a stone's throw from the historic main street of Niagara-on-the-Lake. As one of the oldest structures in the community, it offers a glimpse into the past—just step through its doors and into a nostalgic interior that dates back to the War of 1812 era. The Angel Inn's rooms, with exposed hand-hewn beams and thick plank floors laid in 1815, still echo the sounds of the British soldiers and townsfolk who gathered there for food and drink two centuries ago.

The inn has survived fire, war and two centuries of change and now enjoys the reputation of being one of Canada's most haunted properties. Rather than attempt to hide the presence of the resident ghost, the owners embrace it as a means of tapping into the building's rich history. Plaques posted just outside the front door tell of Captain Colin Swayze, a British officer who met a tragic death on the premises and has since taken up permanent residence, and many staff members are more than willing to discuss their own hair-raising encounters with the supernatural.

Even those uninterested in the paranormal appreciate the building's long, rich history, which dates back to the late 18th century. The inn may have been built as early as 1789, when it was known as the Harmonious Coach House. For many years it was the centre of social activity in the community. Since Niagara-on-the-Lake had been selected as the first capital of Upper Canada, the Harmonious Coach House hosted many important historical figures, including John Graves Simcoe, the first lieutenant-governor of the province, and General Isaac Brock, hero of the War of 1812. But despite such important patrons, most of the inn's clientele consisted of travellers seeking food and shelter and soldiers from nearby Fort George who were all too eager to part with their meagre pay in exchange for whisky and beer. British officers were occasionally billeted at the inn as well.

In December of 1813, Niagara-on-the-Lake was burned to the ground by American forces that had briefly occupied the town. Among the dozens of buildings destroyed was the Harmonious Coach House. All that remained after the winter snows had cooled the ashes was a mound of cinders and blackened bricks. Shortly after the war ended, a second tavern was built upon the fire-scarred foundations of the original. With the new structure came a new name: the Angel Inn, in tender reference to the owner's beloved wife, who he considered heaven-sent. The Angel Inn changed hands many times over the ensuing two centuries, was occasionally known under other names, and at times wasn't even operated as an inn or tavern. The one thing that has remained constant throughout the years has been the mournful presence of Captain Swayze, whose relationship with the inn dates back to the year 1813.

Captain Swayze was a dashing young officer in the British army. He craved glory and advancement, so he was disappointed when in 1812 he was sent to the backwaters of North America to defend Canada instead of being posted to the Duke of Wellington's army fighting Napoleon in Portugal and Spain. His dour mood only darkened when months passed and there were no battles in which he could distinguish himself. To an ambitious young officer, being sent to Canada might have seemed like banishment. He found some solace in the bottom of the bottle and began spending a great deal of time at the Harmonious Coach House. One day he laid eyes on

Euretta, the daughter of the innkeeper, and in that instant the darkness that clouded his spirit was lifted. She was the most beautiful woman the young officer had ever seen. Swayze fell instantly and hopelessly in love.

Over the course of the next few weeks, Swayze devoted much of his energy to gaining first the girl's attention, and then her affection. In time he succeeded, and she too fell deeply in love with him. The two shared a passionate relationship, full of romance and laughter. Swayze imagined a day when the war would be over and he could turn his thoughts from fighting the enemy to establishing a family with the woman he loved. Euretta was all he could think of; her smile haunted his dreams, the aroma of a flower playing upon the breeze reminded him of her scent, and imagining the next time he would feel the warmth of her skin distracted him from daily tasks. The relationship blossomed as the months passed, and it became painful for the lovers to be apart from one another.

Then came the American invasion of May 25, 1813, to shatter their idyllic existence. Swayze watched the enemy cross the Niagara River in overwhelming numbers, intent on capturing Niagara-on-the-Lake and adjacent Fort George. He led his men to oppose them and was soon caught up in the life-and-death struggle that was battle. There were too many invaders, however, and the British had to slowly give ground. Eventually, it became obvious that further resistance was futile. The British commander reluctantly ordered a retreat that abandoned Niagara-on-the-Lake to the enemy.

The love-struck captain panicked. How long would it be before he saw Euretta again? It could be weeks, months, perhaps even years. Passion clouded his judgment; he had to see her one last time, to etch her angelic face in his memory and to extract a promise from her that no matter how long it might be, they would faithfully wait for each other. So while the British forces were in headlong retreat, the young officer lingered behind. Swayze slipped through the shadows of the eerily quiet town, heading for the inn and the arms of his sweetheart.

Unfortunately, American soldiers caught sight of his unmistakable red uniform just as he entered the building and a detachment was sent to capture him. Peering from behind a curtained window, Swayze saw the enemy surrounding the building and knew he was trapped. He briefly considered fighting his way out, cutting a route to freedom with his sword, but he quickly put such thoughts aside. There were simply too many soldiers. Swayze realized there was no hope for escape. His only chance was to hide. With American soldiers pounding on the doors, he raced down to the basement and concealed himself inside an empty barrel.

The enemy burst into the inn and began tearing it apart, searching for the officer they knew hid somewhere within. Swayze's heart raced as the soldiers made their way down to the basement and began thrusting their bayonets into sacks and barrels. Finally, one of the blades found its mark, piercing through wood and imbedding itself deep into Swayze's chest. He tumbled from his hiding spot, crying out for his beloved, his bloodied hands reaching out for her. Euretta pushed through the throng of enemy soldiers and cradled her man in her lap. The last thing Captain Swayze saw as his lifeblood drained from his body was the tear-streaked face of Euretta, tormented by sadness but still lovely.

According to legend, Swayze's body was buried in an unmarked grave in the cellar where he died. But even in death Swayze couldn't be parted from Euretta. He rose from his earthen grave to be reunited with her. Unfortunately, after the inn was burned down later that year, Euretta's father sold the property and moved on. There would be no reunion of young lovers. And yet Swayze, ever faithful, remains at the inn, awaiting the day when Euretta will jump into his arms and smother him with kisses once more.

All manner of inexplicable happenings and mysterious phenomena have been recorded at the Angel Inn over the years. Sometimes these strange things are nothing more than "eerie feelings" that come over staff when they are alone in the building—an indescribable sense that they aren't alone, even though they know there is no one else around. Other times, Captain Swayze is far more obvious in making his presence known.

The hauntings are not a recent phenomenon, but are as old as the building itself. Shortly after John Ross rebuilt the fire-ravaged inn, disembodied footsteps began to interrupt his sleep. The unexplainable late-night wanderings were soon accompanied by other strange noises— a whispered voice, doors groaning as they were opened by invisible hands, screams of pain, creaking stairs. The innkeeper was mystified as to the source of the sounds. Then one night, the culprit was discovered. He was a British officer, misty in form, who wandered the darkened inn as if searching for something or someone.

Since then, Captain Swayze has been blamed for any number of mysterious bumps and other noises that have been heard throughout the building, and for mischievous pranks that leave staff members and guests alike perplexed. Chairs have been propelled across the room, dishes have rattled noisily in the cupboard, the sounds of fife and drums have been heard emanating from an upstairs bedroom. Even today, it's not uncommon for the building's alarm to go off late at night and for the security company to pick up movement on the motion detectors even when the building is empty.

In recent months, there has been an unusual development in Captain Swayze's behaviour. According to experiences reported by a number of guests, the inn's resident spirit has developed a shoe fetish. No matter how scattered they left them the night before, guests awake in the morning to find their shoes neatly lined up. The shoes are lined up in order of size, always in a perfect row, each shoe containing a carefully rolled sock. Eyewitnesses agree it is done with almost military precision. Because these events are recent and not widely known, there's little chance that people are making up these stories for attention, and the stories align too perfectly to be a mere coincidence. Is Captain Swayze, the disciplined military man accustomed to order and uniformity, really tidying up after careless guests? There seems to be no other explanation.

More disturbing was a nighttime visit Swayze made to a young woman staying in one of the inn's second floor guest rooms. The woman, in Niagara-on-the-Lake to attend a conference, checked into the Olde Angel Inn midweek. Jean, the front desk manager, didn't have the heart to tell her that once the lively pub closed and all the bar staff left at 1:00 AM, she would be entirely alone in the building. "I kept that to myself because I thought it would freak her out—it would freak me out being alone in the inn overnight," Jean explains honestly. "Why make her nervous?"

The young woman retired to her room that night and settled into bed. The muted sounds of music and chatter filtered up through the floorboards from the pub below until 1:00 AM, when suddenly the building went completely silent. There were no footsteps across creaking floorboards, no hum of nearby conversations, no sign that there was anyone besides herself in the building. Still, the woman wasn't concerned. She was certain there were other guests sleeping soundly in adjacent rooms or a staff member somewhere below making every effort to be quiet. Soon, she drifted off into contented sleep.

Later that night, she awoke with a start. In the groggy netherworld between awake and asleep she vaguely registered a presence in the room with her. Then as she became more alert she realized someone was gently brushing strands of hair away from her face and lightly caressing her skin. Suddenly wide awake, she bolted upright in bed and, with eyes wide with terror, searched the room for an intruder. To her relief she discovered there was no one there, and the door to her room remained locked. Still, though she realized she was alone and in no danger, the experience left her rattled and as a result she was awake for hours with the blankets pulled protectively to her chin. Every time she would border on falling back to sleep there would be a creaking sound or a faint breeze and she would find herself wide awake again.

"She came down to the lobby in the morning, and as usual I asked if everything was all right and if she had slept well. That was when she told me about her ghostly encounter the night before. I never did tell her that she was all alone in the inn that night. I thought that would only make things scarier for her," explains Jean. "I recounted this tale to a couple who were staying in the same room a couple of weeks later. They were sitting at the bar and when my tale was over the woman burst into tears. She had experienced the same thing!"

Guests staying overnight in the second floor bedrooms will often hear the sounds of a bar in full-swing below them well after the pub has closed for the night and the staff have gone home. One minute they are blissfully dreaming, and the next, sleep is interrupted by merry laughter, muffled conversations, dishes rattling noisily and glasses clinking. Those brave enough to investigate creep warily down the stairs; as soon as they draw near, the noise stops and they find the dining room empty of revellers. Sometimes, just sometimes, the sound of heavy footsteps retreating from the darkened pub and down the stairs to the basement can be heard. Even morning and the arrival of staff cannot guarantee an end to the mysterious phenomena. Table settings will change by themselves, understandably annoying waitresses, and kegs of American beer have a habit of malfunctioning.

While the bedrooms and barroom definitely have had their share of strangeness, the basement is truly the focal point of the inn's ghostly activity. It was there, after all, that Captain Swayze was killed. Perhaps the emotional trauma of his final moments ensures that his spirit is most tightly bound to the place of his violent death. Indeed, many people have commented on the eerie ambience of "Swayze's Cellar"; some patrons are so unnerved that they simply can't descend the stairs. Unnatural, spine-chilling cold spots are felt throughout the basement; the loud clomping of heavy boots upon the age-worn stairs is heard; and the reflection of a red-coated soldier is seen in the mirror in the ladies room. On those few occasions when Captain Swayze's ghostly apparition is seen, it's most often in the basement.

Bethany is another young lady with a frightful story to share. She and her family were visiting the Niagara region as a summer daytrip. They spent the morning seeing the Falls, and then put the crowds and neon lights of Clifton Hill behind them for a more peaceful afternoon in the quaint surroundings of Niagara-on-the-Lake. Where better to enjoy lunch than the historic Olde Angel Inn, they had all agreed, and none of them were disappointed with the food or the atmospheric décor. However, throughout her meal, Bethany couldn't escape the feeling of being watched. She looked around several times to see if another customer or a staff member was looking at her, but the pub was quiet and the few people there seemed uninterested in her. Once, she was even startled to feel a hand on her shoulder. She turned quickly, expecting to find a waitress bringing their check, but there was no one anywhere near her.

Before they left, Bethany elected to use the ladies room in the basement. As she began to descend the stairs she felt an inexplicable lump form in her throat. The staircase is perhaps a bit dimly lit but is in no way sinister, so she couldn't explain her sudden unease. She shrugged it off and continued. Just as she reached the bottom a breeze gusted from the short hallway ahead, blowing Bethany's hair into her face. The wind was cold and clammy. With neither open doors nor air vents in the hall there was no natural source for the breeze; it simply should not have existed. With a startled gasp, Bethany raced back up the stairs, the urgency of using the ladies room quickly forgotten.

But it wasn't in the basement—or anywhere in the building, for that matter—that the most frightening encounter with the long-dead officer occurred. Rather, it was in the street outside. The fog, almost without warning, swirled off of Lake Ontario that early fall evening and settled upon the sleepy village. A guest at the inn, an American tourist who had been skeptical of the supernatural stories surrounding the building and had not been afraid to say so, was just returning from his day of exploring the local attractions when the gloom settled in. He quickened his pace to reach the warmth of the inn, but as he approached he suddenly felt a sense of malice invisibly reaching out for him. His nerves were instantly on edge. Just then a figure appeared in the fog, faint at first, barely a shadowy outline. The figure glided forward—it was a British officer, 200 years dead, his lifeless eyes staring, his mouth opened to speak but making no sound. Shocked into action, the tourist bolted for the Angel Inn, feeling safe only once he was through its doors.

Captain Swayze is usually benign, even friendly, but perhaps the tourist's disbelief of the supernatural, combined with the fact he was an American—the enemy, in Swayze's day—drove him to materialize in so sinister and terrifying a manner.

The Olde Angel Inn is an excellent place to enjoy a drink or a hearty pub-style meal. It's a place dripping in charm and nostalgia, and it's rare to enter and not be greeted by the lively sounds of people enjoying them-selves. This cheerfulness masks the darker side of the building. The inn is, after all, also a tomb for Captain Swayze. His restless spirit is forever tied to the building under which legend says he is buried, the building where he and his beloved Euretta first gazed affectionately into one another's eyes. The captain aches longingly for her, and will faithfully remain there until such time as they are reunited. Tragically, it's his stubborn faithfulness that prevents the couple from being together. If only he would release his hold on the inn and allow his soul to pass through the portal of death, he'd undoubtedly be greeted by her on the other side, arms spread wide and tears of joy streaking down her angelic face.

Lewiston Refugees

A woman stumbles through a world of ice and snow, frozen fingers pressing a sobbing infant to her chest in a feeble attempt to keep her child warm in the biting cold. The wind swirls billows of snow around the pathetic string of refugees struggling along a lonely road, each one, like the woman and her child, fleeing from their burning homes. She shudders from an oppressive feeling of helplessness. Then a strange lethargy steals through her, a kind of weariness she has never experienced before even working dawn to dusk on her farm. The young mother knows she has to save her child, but she doesn't believe she has the strength to continue. She is exhausted and doesn't want to struggle anymore.

Dimly, through her listlessness, she hears an elderly man pleading with his wife. The frail woman has simply sat down in a drift and refused to go any farther, her will to survive sapped by the cold. Realizing his wife can go no farther, the elderly man drops down beside her, wraps his arms around her shoulders and lightly kisses her cheek. They will face the end together, embracing one another as they fall into a sleep from which there is no awaking.

The young mother averts her eyes from the sad scene and trudges sluggishly forward through yet another snow drift. She takes one more step and then pitches forward as her legs, shaking from exhaustion, suddenly give out. For a long moment she thinks of just lying there and going to sleep. The urge to give up is overwhelming. It would be so easy to simply close her eyes and fall asleep. But then she feels her baby move feebly against her chest and hears her sad, plaintive whimper. The spark of life, on the verge of blinking out, is suddenly reignited. A tiny, precious life is in her hands. As long as her child lives, she won't give up. Lifting herself to her knees, then back to her feet, she moves forward. Her heart surges. Despite the snow that stretches ahead for as far as her eyes can see, she knows she will survive.

Dozens of people would not be so lucky. Their lifeless bodies would line the road leading from the ashes of Lewiston like grim memorials to a night of terror. Many of their frozen bodies wouldn't be found until weeks later, some not even until spring, when the melting snow revealed where the fallen had succumbed to the cold. Although they had not been killed in battle, they were nonetheless victims of a war that by the end of 1813 had turned ugly, brutal and pitiless. The shadow forms of these refugees haunt the road to this day, refusing to allow us to forget their suffering and the human cost of war.

In early December, 1813, after a year-long occupation, General George McClure of the U.S. Army decided he had no choice but to abandon Canada's Niagara region and give up his hard-won gains. But before his army retreated back across the Niagara River, he ordered it to lay waste to the countryside and its communities, ensuring that the land the British recovered would be useless. The villages of St. Davids, Queenston and Niagara-on-the-Lake were all burned to the ground, their residents cast out into bitter cold. Weeks later, the people of Lewiston, New York, would pay dearly for McClure's vindictiveness.

Before the ashes of those ravaged communities had even cooled, the enraged British and Canadians began plotting revenge. During the evening of December 18, 1813, British soldiers, Canadian militiamen and allied Native Americans crossed the Niagara River and captured Fort Niagara with barely a shot fired. Then they turned their attention south, toward the sleeping village of Lewiston.

At the time, Lewiston was the social hub of America's Niagara frontier, far eclipsing Buffalo or any other community in the region in size, wealth and importance. It was home to perhaps 200 souls and boasted a thriving commercial centre consisting of several taverns, multiple stores and about a dozen craftsmen. In its day, Lewiston was considered the "Gateway to the West" because all ship-borne cargo and passengers bound for Lake Huron and beyond had to disembark there to portage around the Niagara gorge and its waterfalls. Lewiston had thus far been largely untouched by the war. That was about to change.

In the early morning hours of December 19, the residents of Lewiston were cozy in their homes, sleeping soundly as snow fell heavily outside and wind rattled shutters. The few who stirred did so only long enough to poke the fires in their hearths, watch as flames burst back to life, and then scamper back to bed. A handful of militia guarded the community, but they too huddled in buildings for warmth. All were blissfully ignorant of the enemy who stealthily approached their slumbering village: 900 First Nations warriors followed by hundreds of British-Canadian troops spilling down River Road, all intent on retribution and turning Lewiston into a pile of ashes.

First to arrive were the Native warriors, who fell upon the unsuspecting settlement with barbaric fury. The small militia force put up only a brief resistance before fleeing. The people of Lewiston had only a few minutes' notice before the enemy descended upon them. All would surely have died if not for the timely arrival of friendly Natives from the nearby Tuscarora reservation, who fought desperately against overwhelming odds to hold off the enemy long enough for sleeping residents to be roused and a few valuables thrown into packs before racing off along snow-clogged roads.

Behind them came the screams of those who weren't able to flee before the attackers tore into them like a pack of wolves, or who refused to abandon their homes. They were butchered by the British-allied rampaging Natives. Men and women alike were scalped, one man beheaded. Tormented parents watched helplessly as their children were stalked like prey. One mother endured the agony of seeing her seven-year-old son shot and scalped. The cries of these victims carried upon the wind and drove the fleeing refugees on fast.

Some paused long enough to look over their shoulders when the sky began to light up with an eerie glow as their homes and businesses were put to the torch in revenge for the earlier razing of St. Davids, Queenston and Niagara-on-the-Lake. Children wailed, and husbands wrapped their arms around their wives to offer meager consolation and made hollow promises that all would be well.

There would be nothing for them to return to as Lewiston was burned to the ground; only one building survived the devastation. The exact number of dead within the village will never be known. One American officer, reporting soon after the attack, said that "it is not yet ascertained how many were killed as most of the bodies were thrown into the burning houses and consumed." The number was likely as high as 46.

Meanwhile, as those bodies burned, along the old Ridge Road toiled a steady file of horses, a few wagons and dozens of pathetic civilians, many barefoot and in nightclothes. There could be no rest as the fleeing villagers were pursued by harrying bands of British-allied Natives. There were countless minor skirmishes as these hunters fell upon stragglers. A few armed villagers and the Tuscarora Indians fired volleys to chase them off, yet still the enemy nipped hungrily at the heels of the fleeing refugees.

The hours of trudging through the snow seemed like a miserable eternity. The numbing cold began to penetrate the refugees' clothing, and the wind shrieked like a banshee, cutting to the bone each time it struck. Only one or two people complained. Most bore the ordeal stoically. They struggled through the storm, desperate to reach safety. As the hours passed the trek became a nightmare of abandonment, fear and despair. Lethargy began to set in, and the old and weak began to fall by the side and soon went quiet and unresponsive. Bravely, they accepted their suffering without protest.

Miles and hours later the homeless found shelter at the Tuscarora village. It was only a temporary refuge, however, as soon this village was overrun as well and the refugees were forced to continue their flight. They were joined by dozens of others fleeing farms in the path of the rampaging enemy. It was a motley throng, with hardly a show of military organization to cover their retreat.

The trail they followed was littered with the bodies of those too weak to continue, or too slow to escape the pursuers. The bodies, stiffened, many with staring lifeless eyes, were eventually covered in snow and would not be recovered until weeks or even months later. How many died in the desperate flight? The number littering the trail may have approached the number killed in Lewiston itself. Their shadow-forms, perhaps joined by others who never truly put that march of terror and misery behind, can still be seen today, reliving their panicked journey.

Little about the roads leading out of Lewiston would strike a motorist as odd during daylight hours. But come sunset, especially on cold winter nights when snow blows across the road and clouds mask the moon, they take on a stark and barren appearance, as if something intangible glares out from the darkness. Many of those driving these roads during winter claim there is more to watch out for than ice patches and white-outs—that if one isn't careful they may collide with shimmering men and women straggling along, unconcerned or unaware of speeding vehicles. Many people don't realize that these roads are heavy with supernatural pedestrian traffic, and the sudden appearance of spectral people in their the headlights can lead to screeching breaks, desperate swerves and worse.

No one knows who spotted the phantom refugees first, but soon after the war they began to appear on frosty nights. Sometimes they appear to be very much alive, but most often it's frighteningly apparent that they're long dead. The figures are deathly pale, said to be a slightly luminescent white and vaguely transparent. They appear singly, in pairs or in small groups. These spirits are so preoccupied with their own plight, their senses so dulled by exhaustion and hypothermia, that they have no concern for vehicles sharing the road.

Some motorists have veered out of their lanes to avoid colliding with the pedestrians, while others, too slow to react, pass straight through them. There is no sound of impact, no sickening thud of flesh connecting with metal. There is only an intense cold within the car, so cold it leaves the driver's breath hanging like mist in the air. Looking in the rearview mirror, no body lies sprawled on the asphalt; indeed, there is no sign of the pedestrian at all. Still, even though no one was hurt in the accident, the driver is traumatized by the experience, left shaking with fright and the supernatural cold that chills the vehicle. It's only later, upon researching their experience, that these shaken witnesses learn that these roads are tainted with the tragic deaths of those who perished when they were forced to flee their homes at the height of winter.

Mysterious ghost lights are also a fixture along these roads. Singly or in flittering groups, they hover over lonely stretches of road, dart in front of vehicles and slowly make their way toward some unknown destination. Some remain visible for only a few moments. And yet, the impact these lights have on eyewitnesses can last years. Just ask Shaun.

"I was driving home late one night, with my dog sleeping in the back seat. There were flurries that night, but the weather wasn't all that bad so I was driving at a steady clip. I came upon these white orbs in the middle of the road that seemed to weave around themselves. There were four or five—it was hard to tell because they were small and fast, and because my attention was also on the road. At first I thought it was just the lights of my car reflecting on the snow, but they got bigger and brighter the closer they got. And then I actually hit them. The car was filled with a blinding light. I had to blink a few times to clear my vision. Then my dog started barking non-stop. He's a little mutt and his yapping is pretty high-pitched, but it sounded extra agitated. He sounded kind of scared. I thought it was just the sudden light, so I wasn't concerned. I was more concerned with my vision, which had those colours you get after looking at light bulb. Then I heard my dog whimper. I looked in the rearview mirror and he looked like he was getting picked up from the stomach. He even made a growling noise. Maybe that startled the spirit because my dog fell to the seat as if released. By this point my dog and I were both scared. I can't get that experience out of my head."

If Shaun thought his experience was frightening, he should talk with a woman who asked that her name be withheld but whom we'll call Anna. Years ago, Anna lived on the rural outskirts of Lewiston, a few miles from the community on a sizeable country lot. Although she had lived there for years, she had never heard of the story surrounding the burning of Lewiston. One night she received a terrifying history lesson.

It was winter, a few days before Christmas. Anna listened as the wind rattled her windows and frosted the panes. She pulled the comforter up close to her chin in an attempt to ward off the unusual feeling that tickled the back of her neck, a sensation that told her something wasn't right. She couldn't place the cause, nor could she shake it. Although the ancient furnace rumbled and a roaring fire crackled in the hearth, the house felt so cold it gnawed through to her bones.

Dimly, over the howl of the wind, Anna heard a strange sound from somewhere in the night. It sounded like a chorus of cries. She crawled from the couch and went to the window, straining her ears to hear more clearly. Then, just as suddenly and unexpectedly as the strange sound first came to her, it faded. It was only her imagination, she told herself, probably nothing more than the wind changing direction and making a different howl through the trees.

Anna returned to the couch and had just settled herself under her blankets when she heard the sound again, briefly, before it died. Something was out there in the blizzard. Anna walked across her floor and stood at the window looking out across her rural lot toward the road. At first she saw nothing through the darkness and the snowflakes. Suddenly, she tensed and squinted her eyes. Something seemed to be moving out there, a vague shape largely obscured by the opaque veil that fell from the sky. She could tell it was moving toward her, and then a gust obliterated it. Her heart stopped beating. A few moments later the shape reappeared, but closer this time. Now she could see that it was a man and a woman huddled against one another, covered in ice and snow. They were pitiful, and for a second Anna thought they might have been in an accident and made their way to her home for help. She ran to her door and opened it.

But as they continued moving sluggishly toward her, Anna realized there was no assisting them. They were gaunt and hard, with flesh as pale as milk. Clearly, they were dead and had been dead for a long, long time. They wore threadbare clothes from another era, and the woman nestled a dark bundle against her chest that Anna believes was a baby wrapped in blankets. The wraiths continued to approach her home in their slow, ungainly walk. Anna's heart stopped in her chest. For a moment she dared not breathe, as if doing so would draw their attention. This was no figment of her imagination. This was real, terrifyingly real.

Finally, the bitter cold wind cutting painfully across her exposed face, hands and feet seemed to snap her back to reality. She slammed the door shut, bolted it locked and raced back to the couch, where she dove under the blankets. There, completely hidden and curled up in a protective ball, she listened. Other than branches stirring in the wind, scratching at one another with wooden fingers, she heard nothing. But she dared not look. What if the ghosts had simply passed through her door and were warming themselves by the fire? She'd rather not know. And so she remained under the blankets, unmoving and scarcely daring to breathe until the morning sun shone through the windows.

Anna and Shaun, like others before them, discovered first-hand that spectral remnants of those who fled the burning of Lewiston two centuries ago continue their desperate attempt to outrun their attackers. Most journeys have an end. Theirs doesn't.

When flurries of wind-borne snow lash the landscape, keep your eyes open if you are travelling the roads around Lewiston at night. You may suddenly find your headlights filled by dishevelled and desperate people walking sluggishly along the road, their thin clothes meager protection from the cold, despair clouding their faces. Don't panic—it's just the ghosts of the tragic Lewiston refugees seeking shelter from the enemy and the elements. But don't stop to offer assistance either. They're long past help, and unless you want your sleep to be interrupted by nightmares, it's best simply to drive by. There's nothing anyone alive can do to ensure they reach safety. The refugees' pitiful flight is doomed to continue forever.

Fort Willow

There is something dark and mysterious about Fort Willow, a partially recreated War of 1812 fortification and supply depot located on the outskirts of the remote and timeless Minesing Swamp. Walking through the gates, you can almost hear the sounds of musket fire and the marching boots of parading soldiers, the echoes of a long-ago war. It is perhaps no wonder that rumours of hauntings should bedevil this place. It is certainly an appropriate setting for a ghost story. The forest here is dark and dense, and the trees' twisted boughs weave a tangled mesh rivalling even the most snaring of spider webs.

When war was declared in 1812 on Britain by the young United States, the U.S. confidently predicted a quick and almost bloodless conquest of British North America, as Canada was then called. That wasn't to be, but the U.S. Navy did seize control of Lake Erie, cutting British communication with her isolated forces on Lake Huron and points farther west. With the majority of her forces tied up fighting Napoleon in Europe, England did not have the option of retaking control of the lake, at least not in the short term.

To skirt American naval supremacy on Lake Erie, and desperate for an alternate means of supplying their garrisons in the west, the British took advantage of an old overland route from Toronto to Lake Huron that had been used for centuries by Native Americans and fur traders. The route travelled up the Humber River to Holland Landing, from which point supplies and personnel were transferred into boats to traverse Lake Simcoe to the site of modern Barrie. There, the Nine Mile Portage led through the wilderness to Willow Creek, which fed into the Nottawasaga River and thence into Lake Huron at Wasaga Beach. Even though the route was less than ideal for military purposes—narrow paths snaked through imposing wilderness, down rivers incapable of supporting large craft, and through a dense swamp every bit as forlorn as Florida's Everglades—it was the best of the available options, and for two years supported British military efforts in the Northwest.

To facilitate the Nine Mile Portage's use for the transport of supplies, significant resources were devoted to improving it over the winter of 1812–1813. The trail was widened and stumps were painstakingly removed to ease the passage of carts and cannons, and for the first time it took on the appearance of a road as we know it. So important was this endeavour that it took precedence over all other war-related industries for a time, including that of building warships—some 300 men were brought in from the naval base at Kingston to help construct the road to Willow Creek.

At the same time, a fort was hacked out of the wilderness at the end of the portage trail to protect the route. Fort Willow, as it was known, consisted of several log barracks, a barn, an officers' cabin and two blockhouses (strong points for defence), surrounded by a stout palisade measuring 180 feet by 250 feet, and beyond that was a string of earthworks and trenches. The garrison numbered 250 men at its peak, including 20 Royal Navy shipwrights brought in to build bateaux (45-foot-long rowboats) for service on the river and Lake Huron.

The backbreaking exertion of building Fort Willow and improving the Nine Mile Portage was not wasted. Both the fort and the road proved vital to keeping Fort Mackinac, an isolated stronghold on Lake Huron and the key to the west, supplied and its garrison fed. Without relief, Mackinac may well have fallen and the outcome of the war been far different. At the very least, Canada beyond the shores of Georgian Bay would likely have been lost permanently to the United States. Despite their valued contribution to the successful war effort, Fort Willow and the Nine Mile Portage were merely expediencies required to carry on the conflict. When peace was signed at the end of 1814, the British abandoned the isolated fort. The soldiers who had garrisoned the fort and endured misery for months on end were pulled out, all save for one unlucky—and ghostly—soldier, who continued to stand sentry over the fort even as the forest reclaimed the site.

He's there still, performing his duty with unflinching and undying devotion. Fort Willow has been partially reconstructed and is part of a conservation area popular with hikers and history buffs alike. Several signs and maps have been erected on site, detailing the history and importance of the fort and the painstaking efforts to rebuild it. A fresh palisade stretches around two-thirds of the site, and foundations for the original buildings have been laid out. Outside the palisade, anyone searching among the trees may be rewarded by stumbling upon the earthworks hurriedly dug to defend the fort. As the site was made more accessible and reconstruction proceeded in the past few decades, sightings of the spectral soldier naturally increased.

A spectral soldier still stands guard over Fort Willow.

"I used to walk my dogs at Fort Willow a lot. It's quiet and I could let the dogs run free, so they enjoyed it as much as I did," relates Gloria. "But I had an experience one day that really unnerved me, and now I won't go back without my husband."

It was an overcast day in early spring. There was still snow on the ground, and breath came in icy trendrils that hung in the air. Gloria had let her German shepherds off their leashes and they tore off in excitement, leaving her temporarily alone. "Suddenly, I felt as if I was being watched by a man from the woods; somehow I just knew it was a man. I was nervous, obviously, and began searching the shadows for someone hiding. I didn't see anyone, but the feeling of fear intensified."

Understandably shaken, Gloria wanted to leave and called for her dogs to return. That's when she saw her mysterious voyeur. "He was kind of see-through, but not misty as you imagine ghosts to be, and I could only see him out of the corner of my eye. If you looked directly at him, somehow you couldn't see him. Then my dogs returned and started acting crazy. They were baring their teeth and snarling and barking in the ghost's direction. I left and didn't look back."

The ghost was described as being a young man, probably no more than a teenager, wearing a 19th-century military uniform. Others who have witnessed the apparition describe him as fair and lanky, with a childlike innocence that seems at odds with the soldierly garb he wears. But who was this ghost in life? Why did he linger even after the fort had been abandoned?

History is largely silent about the subject, which isn't surprising; Fort Willow was an obscure posting in an obscure war. The soldier certainly wouldn't have died as a result of hostile action, since Fort Willow was far from the front lines. However, it's possible and indeed quite likely that he—and perhaps others—succumbed to disease or ailments there and were buried in graves long since grown over. Fort Willow was, after all, described as a "malarial" and "hellish" swamp in summer and completely isolated in winter.

Where history leaves off, legend takes over. It was the winter of 1813–1814. For the soldiers stationed at forlorn Fort Willow, the war seemed to be an endless misery without respite. The weather was brutal and unforgiving. Thigh-high blankets of snow made walking an almost impossible chore, and howling winds bit through the soldiers' greatcoats, cutting to the bone. Temperatures dipped so low that it proved impossible to warm the barracks.

The chill was always with the soldiers and they soon forgot what it felt like to be warm. There was scant warmth to be found at Fort Willow; the walls were cold, and their commanding officer even colder.

Among the soldiers enduring this ordeal was a young private, barely more than a boy and so far from home. Over the course of this winter that seemed to stretch on forever, the private was stricken with sickness and fever. Perhaps knowing that his end was near, he began weeping and calling desperately for his mother. Over and over again the young man cried out, pleading to once again hear the voice of his mother, or to feel the warmth of her arms around him, to lay eyes upon the home in which he was raised from birth. Weakened by illness, he looked more child than soldier. The need to return home had become overwhelming, and as the end neared, his sobbing became more desperate. Fever induced delirium, and one night the soldier pulled himself from his bunk and set out under the cover of darkness to be reunited with his mother.

With the rising of the morning sun his absence was noticed. Search parties set out after him. Slowed by weakness due to illness and the deep snow, he hadn't gotten far. His mates quickly caught up to him. He was staggering through the snow, clinging to trees for support, more dead than alive. They carried their ill comrade-in-arms back to the barracks, threw warm blankets over him and did their best to comfort him.

There was no such sympathy from Fort Willow's commanding officer, however. The captain was furious. No one disobeyed him, certainly not a lowly private. He felt that a strong message had to be sent so others wouldn't attempt to desert, so he ordered a strong punishment. The young soldier was lashed ruthlessly, and when the last of his strength had nearly expired, a rope was knotted around his neck and he was hauled to the top of the flagpole for all to see. His legs kicked violently for what must have seemed like an eternity as his own body weight slowly strangled him. Just as his body twitched for the last time the young man cried out, "Why?"

For several days the body remained hanging from the top of the pole. When it was finally brought down, its ghastly appearance sent a bone-chilling shudder through the other soldiers. The eyes were eaten away, and the disfigured head rolled to one side. The soldiers said a simple prayer for their dead comrade and then buried him in a grave just outside the palisade. A year later the garrison pulled out, never to return, never knowing that they had left someone—even if only in spirit—behind.

Echoes of fear, sadness and confusion taint this mostly forgotten fort.

Today, the spectral soldier walks silently beneath the partially reconstructed palisade and through the regenerated woods. In some witnesses he invokes fear, in others sadness at the terrible suffering he endured in his final moments, and in still others disorientation and confusion. These feelings are no doubt reflections of those the young soldier himself experienced as he was sentenced to death for a crime he didn't commit. And while he may not intend harm, in at least one case the undead soldier's presence was accompanied by painful stiffening in the witness' neck that lasted for almost an hour after the encounter.

Needless to say, few people visit Fort Willow after dark. Surrounded by dark woods with only the pale light of the moon to illuminate the grounds, the fort can be creepy enough without the wraith of a murdered man slinking from tree to tree. But back in the early 2000s, a couple, engrossed in walking the trails, failed to notice the deepening shadows. By the time they made it back to the fort, twilight was upon them. So too, they would soon discover, was a long-dead soldier who had clawed his way up from a long-forgotten grave.

They were just about to pass through the fort on their way back to the parking lot and their waiting car when the woman reached out and grabbed hold of her companion's arm, drawing him to a halt. Her stare was fixated on the fort. "Something's not right here. There's someone here, watching us," she said, her voice small and far away. "Can't you feel it?"

The wind ruffled the foliage momentarily, but nothing else moved. The couple stood close to one another, staring through the gate of the fort, trying to detect the entity they sensed waiting within. Their eyes strained, but there was only more of what they had already seen—the foundations of former buildings, the log palisade with a Union Jack flying over it, and a dense, rapidly darkening forest encroaching upon it on all sides.

"There's nothing here," said the man, trying to sound brave and reassuring, though hardly feeling it himself. "I think it's all good."

His companion knew different. She could feel a presence, life beyond that of nature. She could feel his eternal torture. She fixed her companion with a haunting gaze, her voice becoming rough and thick with fear: "He's out there, watching. He keeps saying, over and over again, 'Why? Why me?' He can't understand why he was hanged and left to die. He was only a boy. He's confused and very angry." She looked back to the fort. The day was beginning to fade toward nightfall; the sun was already below the trees. "We shouldn't be here," she said suddenly, terror rising within her.

Feet barely touched ground as they raced to their car. As they drove out onto the gravel road, the friends let out their breaths like long hisses, letting the pent-up tension escape. The fear of the moment slowly drained away, leaving them exhausted and relieved.

But the woman could not easily shake the experience. She felt as dark and lost as did the ghost, and only slowly did the spirit's cold embrace leave her. Even as the chill left her body, it was replaced by an agonizingly stiff neck that lingered for days and made it almost impossible to straighten her head into an upright position. Was her sore neck some sort of psychic reflection of the manner in which the young soldier died?

Fort Willow is undoubtedly one of Ontario's hidden gems, a location rich in history, recreational opportunities and natural splendour ideal for wildlife watchers. Its soaring trees, gravel walking paths, informative plaques and wooden palisade, all surrounded by a chorus of bird calls, belie its darker side, for time has not exorcised its ghost. There are times when the birds suddenly fall silent, when the forests grow strangely sinister, and an unnatural cold frosts the leaves. It's at these times that a shadow separates itself from the gloom of the woods and takes on the form of a long-dead soldier who roams aimlessly around the deserted fort. His emotions are in turmoil, a turbulent brew of anger, confusion, sadness and suffering, and as a result, when he encounters mortals the result can be unpredictable, even terrifying and painful. But he's an entity that deserves our sympathy, for his life was cut short by a tragic mistrial of justice.

Like the winter endured by soldiers at this frontier posting, stories about Fort Willow's ghost are chilling. Ice runs down your spine as you listen to the otherworldly encounters with the undead Redcoat. They are tales that should be told only on a pleasant summer day, or at least beside a roaring fire with a hot mug of something to steady the nerves. Almost two centuries have passed, and yet the young soldier can find no lasting peace. He remains tied to Fort Willow, perhaps attempting to prove—for all eternity, if need be—that he did not knowingly desert his post all those years before.

Bird Island Lighthouse

The sea is a dangerous, even sinister place, where powerful storms overwhelm unsuspecting ships and hidden rocks and shoals rip open hulls. Mariners know better than anyone the primal power of the world's oceans and man's helplessness in the face of nature's fury. Consequently, the beam of a lighthouse cutting through the night's gloom has been a comforting sight to sailors since maritime travel began. Whereas the seas want to claim lives, it is the job of lighthouses to help to save them. These beacons are symbols of hope and protection, like white angels perched on rocky islands surrounded by angry waters. And yet, despite the countless lives they have saved, some lighthouses are grief-stricken spots.

As the sun sets on Sippican Harbor in Buzzards Bay off of Marion, Massachusetts, a light appears on Bird Island. It's not the welcome flash of the Bird Island Lighthouse, which guided sailors for over 100 years but is no longer operational. Rather, it's a pale glow flitting along the shore of the uninhabited two-acre rock. If you were to grab binoculars to get a better view, or hop into a boat to investigate, you would see the form of an aged woman walking along the isle's rocky coast, glowing pale blue as if under the pall of a full moon. Get close enough and you might hear her cries as she mourns her own death and the fact that she remains imprisoned on the isolated island with only seabirds as companions. She's been there as long as the lighthouse has stood, enduring centuries of loneliness and despair. Her name is Sarah Moore, and she suffers in death as deeply as she did in life.

Bird Island Lighthouse was built in 1819. The first keepers were Sarah and her husband, William (or Bill, as he was more commonly called) Moore. Bill was as unpredictable as an Atlantic gale, and just as violent. Most of the time, he vented his temper on his long-suffering wife. A conniving and dastardly sort, he hated honest work and preferred to make his money through less than honourable means. Why callous one's hands or endure long, mind-numbing hours at a desk when it was so much easier to earn a living by fleecing people, conning them or even stealing from them? That was his philosophy, and it served him well because in the years leading up to the War of 1812 he had maintained a comfortable lifestyle and won the hand of a beautiful woman from an upper-class Boston family.

When the war broke out, Bill saw an opportunity too tempting to pass up. War, after all, has always presented opportunities for profiting, and he intended to line his pockets even as battles raged and thousands died. History isn't certain exactly what his scheme was, only that it was unsavoury and quite successful. Some people claim he was a government-sanctioned privateer who decided it was simpler to turn pirate and prey upon ships of all flags, including American. Others—and there are records that seem to support them—say he was an army paymaster who pocketed some of the money meant for the soldiers doing the grim duty of fighting the enemy. According to this version, he was caught red-handed and discharged in disgrace. One thing is certain: by the end of the war he owed the U.S. War Department money and his reputation was in tatters. Whether it was thievery on the high seas or from the army on campaign, Bill Moore had to pay for his crimes.

Bill's punishment was to serve as keeper of the new Bird Island lighthouse. His sentence was undetermined, certainly for a number of years until the government decided he had worked off his debt. When he first looked upon Bird Island, Moore's heart sank into his stomach. A barren, windswept rock surrounded by seas often whipped into a violent frenzy, it looked worse than any brick and mortar prison he could imagine. He wasn't even trusted with a boat, lest the temptation prove too much and he use the boat to escape. Instead, food and other supplies were brought to the isolated island on a scheduled basis. The prison wasn't his alone: his wife, Sarah, would share his fate.

The island seemed cursed from the start. The first winter brought a severe gale. The intensity of the storm swept away everything on the island that wasn't secured. The frightened light keeper and his wife had to retreat to the tower as white caps of the freezing cold waters threatened to envelop their home. The island remained under water for much of the day, and as they were trapped in the tower Bill began to realize just how tortured an existence on this god-forsaken rock would be.

Worse, as he looked on the face of his aging wife, haggard and tired, an ever-present corncob pipe clenched between her teeth, he started to think of his marriage as a torture as well. He had married a beautiful young woman, but now Sarah was as craggy-featured and grey as Bird Island. Bill finally admitted to himself that he hated her; perhaps he had never loved her at all, but only the idea of a pretty wife who could be shown off and make other men envious. In a fit of rage, he took hold of her pipe and smashed it against the wall. "It's a filthy habit," he said through clenched teeth. Sarah simply looked at him, her eyes devoid of emotion.

As the years passed and isolation on the island took its toll, Bill's temper grew worse. He began to blame Sarah for his plight; he convinced himself that he had sunk to thievery to provide the luxuries and standard of living his wife, the daughter of a well-to-do family, demanded of him. Whenever his mood turned black, Bill would beat mercilessly on his mate.

A small, frail woman, Sarah could do little to defend herself and could only endure the abuse as best she could. People on the mainland suspected what was going on, but what could they do? They had no proof, after all, and Sarah never raised a word of complaint. All she meekly asked for was pipe tobacco, which her husband denied her out of resentment. "That damn pipe will be the death of her," he would mutter darkly. As a demonstration of sympathy, mainlanders would hide packs of tobacco in with the supplies delivered to the island. She deserved that much, they reasoned.

The island was a prison of misery for both husband and wife for more than a decade. Out of his mind with hatred, Bill began to plot the end of his tormenter's life. At first it was merely a fantasy, but the more he thought about it, the more attractive the idea became to him. *She deserves to die for making my life a living hell*, he thought. *And if I go to hell for killing her, it wouldn't be any worse than what I've endured already.*

Finally, in 1832, with the deadly plan fully formed in his deranged mind, Bill built up the courage to follow through. Gun in hand, he stalked his wife across the island, finally spotting her walking along the rocky shoreline, gazing out to sea, the ever-present corncob pipe dangling from her lips. *That damn pipe. I always said it would kill her*, he laughed to himself sinisterly. Bill snuck up behind his wife, levelled the pistol behind her head and pulled the trigger. The bark of the gun echoed across the bay and Sarah dropped lifelessly, her blood seeping down the rocks and into the Atlantic waters. Bill was shaking all over. In some ways he was relieved, as if he was tasting freedom for the first time in years. He felt as though he was waking from a nightmare. Sarah's glassy, dead eyes stared up at him accusingly as he placed her body in a shallow grave and covered it with earth and rock.

Bill's plan was not yet complete. He had no intention of going to prison or, worse yet, being hanged, for murder. He raised the distress flag to call authorities to the island. When they arrived, Bill called down to them from the door of his home. Sarah had died from tuberculosis, he yelled, and he feared he had contracted the illness as well. The authorities, not wanting to catch the contagious disease, nervously backed away and returned to their boat. They took his word and intended to leave it at that.

Over the following days and weeks, word of Sarah's death spread and sat uncomfortably with many of the locals who had long suspected that Bill abused his wife. Everyone suspected murder and pleaded with authorities to return to the island. Finally giving in to the pressure, law officers headed out to Bird Island to question the light keeper. They found the rock devoid of life. Bill Moore had disappeared without a trace. How could he have escaped from the island? It's known that Moore occupied some of his time on Bird Island performing experiments aimed toward perfecting "air boxes." These were intended to be built into ships to keep them from sinking, but they just as likely could float a person away from the island in the dark of the night without being seen.

Regardless of how he engineered his escape, Bill Moore was never seen again and so his crime went unpunished. Perhaps that is why the spirit of his wife, Sarah Moore, haunts the scene of her brutal murder. It wasn't long after her death that keepers began to complain of frightening occurrences during their tenure on Bird Island. On overcast days, when grey clouds hang low in the sky and a cold drizzle falls from above, they claimed to see the ghostly manifestation of a sad-looking woman wandering the island, looking out to sea as if searching for something, or perhaps someone.

Night provided little comfort for the restless spirit. One night, the lighthouse keeper who replaced Bill Moore heard a light rapping on the door of his cabin. At first he thought it was merely the rattling of the wind, but the rapping became louder, more insistent, more obviously the sound of someone knocking. Maybe a ship had gone down, he thought in a panic. Worried that a half-drowned, freezing sailor had crawled ashore, he raced to the door with a thick blanket in hand. When he opened it, to his horror he came face to face with an old woman, her skin as pale as milk. Her mouth moved to speak, but no words came. The keeper recoiled, stepping back from the walking corpse. The woman turned from the door and walked toward the sea. She stopped once, turning back toward the keeper with a pitiful look on her face. She reached out to him with an outstretched hand, but when the frightened lighthouse keeper didn't move to take it, she continued her lonely walk to the shore, slowly fading into nothingness.

The visitations became frequent, most often on the night of the full moon. The keeper's family began to dread the unearthly knock. It became a portent of terror and they refused to answer, knowing well it was Sarah Moore's ghost looking for her alleged murderer. Subsequent keepers endured similar nighttime torment.

A remarkable discovery was made in 1889 when the original lighthouse keeper's house was torn down to make room for a new, more spacious and modern home. When the warped floorboards of the weathered old structure were removed, workers were startled to find a rusting flintlock pistol, which many locals believed to be the weapon used to kill Sarah Moore. Alongside the gun was a small leather pouch containing tobacco and a folded piece of yellowed paper. The note, written by William Moore, seemed to be intended to absolve his soul of blame for Sarah's death. In it, he blamed certain local residents for supplying the tobacco that put "a dreadful end to my dearly loved wife."

No one bought it, especially not the restless spirit of Sarah Moore herself. Far from finding any peace after the discovery was made, her ghost became more active. It was as if she was demanding that the relics be used as evidence to bring her murderer to justice, unaware that her husband was almost certainly moldering in his own grave by then.

Keeper after keeper would cringe at the faint rapping on the door, knowing what unearthly figure stood beyond its threshold. Those new to the island would answer the door upon hearing the knocking and instantly regret doing so. Some would find the entrance empty of any form. In those instances, the smell of tobacco hung thickly in the ocean air and an unnatural cold, unlike any breeze coming in off the Atlantic, would chill them. Others came face to face with Sarah herself. She would reach out to them with ethereal hands, her face a mask of unfathomable sadness. But while their hearts may have gone out to the spectral woman, the keepers were always so frightened that they slammed the door and latched it securely.

Not that such measures did much good; in time Sarah's mist-like form began appearing within the house as well, floating across rooms and leaving the musty odor of tobacco in her wake. As more decades passed and she grew despondent of ever finding the peace that only justice could bring, Sarah's spirit grew increasingly active and no place on the island was safe from her manifestations. Needless to say, many keepers were relieved when they were released from their tour of duty at the haunted beacon.

Bird Island Lighthouse was finally decommissioned on June 15, 1933, when the Cape Cod Canal and its lighted buoys had made the decrepit signal obsolete. The only inhabitants on the island from that point on were nesting sea birds and the apparition of an old woman wandering among the deserted buildings. Within a few years, the roof of the keeper's home had collapsed into ruin, adding to the island's haunted reputation. A hurricane that devastated the Atlantic Seaboard in 1938 destroyed every building on the island except for the light tower itself. But while the crashing waves and gale-force winds may have swept wood and brick out to sea, Sarah Moore's ghost clung to the rocks and her soul remained firmly anchored to the island where she was killed and her body buried.

In the decades following, sailors and fishermen aboard vessels passing close by Bird Island would often see a woman walking forlornly along the water's edge. She looked so real, so lifelike, that some even thought she was in distress—perhaps the survivor of a boat that went down—and went to render assistance. As the mariners closed in and called out to her, Sarah would simply look at them with the saddest eyes they had ever seen and fade away into nothingness.

A pair of fishermen saw Sarah in the summer of 1982. She was still walking—or more properly, as the men stressed, floating—along the shores, sad and lonely, scanning the horizon for signs of her murderous husband. When last they saw her before their boat pulled out of sight, Sarah was still weeping and wandering aimlessly. In more recent years, people have sometimes claimed to see lights burning in the island's lighthouse, even though its light has long been extinguished. Is this Sarah drawing attention to herself by hailing passing boats? Is she worried that her story is being forgotten?

By 1997, the 178-year-old lighthouse was crumbling, with loose mortar and broken glass perched precariously atop an unstable foundation. It was clear that the battering of Atlantic storms would one day soon topple the aging structure. The Sippican Historical Society mobilized to prevent this from occurring. They knew that the Bird Island lighthouse was one of the oldest original lighthouse structures in North America and deserved to be preserved. With the assistance of the Town of Marion, the Historical Society made extensive renovations on the structure to stabilize and restore it. Bird Island was added to the National Registrar of Historic Places and opened to the public. While visitors cannot enter the lighthouse itself, they can stand at its base and gaze up at the majestic tower, and perhaps reflect on the lonely existence of those charged with maintaining the light in a past era.

Sarah Moore is still trapped there, occasionally seen beckoning to passing boats with a pleading, outstretched hand. The sad look on her face is a reflection of the despair of her final years and the untimely nature of her demise. Undeath itself seems to possess an innate sadistic streak. How else do you explain that those who have suffered most in life should find their agony prolonged even after that tragic life has ended. Here she is, almost 200 years since her murder at the hands of her cruel husband, and she is still tormented. Every day is a nightmare for her as she relives a life of abuse and a violent death. The poor woman is imprisoned on this barren rock by the vast stretch of water that surrounds it and by the nature of her death, both of which prevent her passing over into a peaceful afterlife.

An unresolved crime is torment to a soul. Only after justice has been served will the ghost pass over to the other side. Unfortunately, it doesn't seem likely Sarah Moore will ever find the justice that is her due. And so she suffers, daily and eternally. She is a benign and gentle soul, but her spirit is also filled with grief and resentment. So if you intend to visit Bird Island, try to avoid cold and stormy days, and above all ensure you are long gone before night descends like a black curtain. You don't want to risk running into the wraith of Sarah Moore. The passage of time has cooled her anger, but one can never be too careful with the dead.

Ghosts of Fort George

No visit to Niagara-on-the-Lake, and no study of War of 1812-era ghosts, is complete without a tour of the historic Fort George National Historic Site, where soldiers, militiamen and Native peoples fought and died 200 years ago. Countless stories have emerged over the years to suggest that the location is rich in not only history but also the paranormal.

In 1796, the British began work on Fort George on the shores of the Niagara River just before it empties into Lake Ontario. Labourers slaved for years on end, working under the glare of American gunners standing upon the walls of Fort Niagara on the opposite side of the river. Finally completed in 1802, Fort George housed a British army garrison and personnel of the Indian Department. At the time, Niagara-on-the-Lake was the provincial capital and Fort George was a cultured and civilized place. The officers of the garrison, men from the upper crust of British society, hosted elegant dinners and balls, staged plays for the public, offered the services of military bands to play concerts, and brought refinement to what would otherwise have been a rough frontier community.

But as tensions between Britain and the United States mounted over the next decade, it became increasingly apparent that the sturdiness of Fort George's walls would be tested by shot and shell. When war erupted in 1812, Fort George became a vital lynchpin of Britain's Niagara defences. During the Battle of Queenston Heights on October 13, 1812, American gunners at Fort Niagara fired hundreds of shells at Fort George, setting several buildings on fire and inflicting casualties amongst her garrison.

Worse was to come the following year when, on May 25, 1813, as a prelude to another American invasion, the dozens of guns from Fort Niagara and those of a fleet anchored in the mouth of the Niagara River opened a thunderous bombardment upon Fort George that showered the greatly outgunned British fortification with shells. Fort George was virtually destroyed by the weight of artillery fire: the walls of its brick buildings crumbled under the pounding; wooden palisades splintered like toothpicks; and fires started by red-hot cannon balls raged uncontrolled. Within a few hours every building in the fort was destroyed—except the stone powder magazine, which survives today as the oldest building in Niagara-on-the-Lake.

With the fort rendered defenceless there was little to oppose the American invasion two days later, on May 27. The rubble-strewn grounds of Fort George were occupied by the American army and used as a base for pushing farther into Upper Canada. It was to be a short-lived occupation, however. The Americans were defeated in two separate battles later in 1813—the Battle of Stoney Creek and the Battle of Beaver Dams—and were forced to retreat back across the Niagara River. Fort George was retaken by British forces in December and partially rebuilt by the British soldiers and Canadian militia that moved in as its garrison.

When the War of 1812 drew to a close, Fort George was abandoned in favour of Fort Mississauga and Butler's Barracks, both located in Niagara-on-the-Lake. The fort was reoccupied during the Rebellion of 1837 and the Fenian Raids of the 1860s, but otherwise was neglected and stood empty. By the turn of the century nothing but the earthworks and stone powder house remained.

Salvation for the fort came during the Depression of the 1930s when the government, desperate to generate tourism and create jobs, decided to rebuild Fort George. Construction was completed in 1940. The fort that emerged from the make-work program and that stands today is a near-perfect replica of how it would have appeared during the War of 1812. Visitors can tour the Soldiers' Barracks, where the wives and children of the soldiers shared the same living space as the men; experience the culture of the Officers' Quarters, where upper class English officers lived a much more elegant lifestyle; observe craftsmen at work in the Artificer's Shop; and linger in the Cookhouse to watch as costumed staff prepare period foods.

Restless spirits of soldiers lurk just out of sight at Fort George.

It is one of Niagara's most popular tourist attractions, but all is not right at Fort George. The stains of blood spilled and lives taken are not easily washed away despite the passage of years, and as the sun sets and long shadows are cast into sinister corners, the dead begin to stir. Restless spirits of soldiers lurk just out of sight of admiring tourists, doomed to remain forever tied to the fort they garrisoned in life. In fact, these ghostly remnants are so common within the wooden walls and earthen parapet that Fort George is widely considered one of the most haunted places in Canada. Certainly, it seems that every one of its buildings has played host to a chilling tale or two.

Rather than focus on the entirety of the fort's ghastly garrison, in this chapter we'll introduce you to two prominent members of this undead army. The first, a tortured spirit known for frightening people with its spooky antics, haunts the location of the former hospital, leading many people to suspect that he may have been an ill-fated patient or even a physician scarred by the horrific wounds he witnessed. The other is the spirit of a young lieutenant or captain who resides within the relative lap of luxury that is the Officers' Quarters. But despite the comfort with which he is surrounded, this ghostly officer is just as tortured, just as trapped between two worlds, as any of the restless soldiers said to be imprisoned within the walls of Fort George.

Former Gift Shop

With all the battles and bloodshed that occurred within the walls of Fort George, it's little wonder that unusual activities take place at this historic site. And yet one of the most haunted locations is also perhaps the most unlikely: a modest frame structure that until very recently housed the fort's gift shop and today serves as a staff kitchen. During its time as a gift shop it was a cheerful building with shelves full of books and other war memorabilia. Here the smiles of staff members would greet visitors as they shopped for mementos of a fun-filled day exploring Canada's military past. But what these tourists don't know, what park staff rarely discussed with the public, was that the gift shop had a long tradition of unexplained paranormal activity. It must have come as quite a shock whenever a whispered voice was heard, or an item suddenly flew off a shelf, or one stepped into a cold spot so chilled it caused goose bumps to crawl over flesh even on a hot summer's day.

Let's take a step back in time to explore the possible origins of this haunting. The building that until recently housed souvenirs related to the war stands on the location of the former garrison hospital, which was built in 1799 while Fort George was still in its infancy. A rumour circulates today that the hospital's basement was where gravely wounded or terminally ill soldiers were sent to die so they were not occupying valuable bed space or unnerving other patients with their last cries of suffering. However, though it makes for a great story, there is simply no truth behind it.

"Nevertheless, while this is an urban legend, there's no doubt that the hospital was a grim place, especially when surgeons were tending to battle wounds. To be sure, there were soldiers who did not recover and would have died here," says Ron Dale, a Parks Canada employee and a published expert on the War of 1812.

As Dale says, soldiers certainly did die in the hospital. Although many of the earliest headstones in nearby St. Mark's Cemetery have been worn smooth by the passage of years and the relentless assault of the elements, several stones still bear witness to the limits of period medicine against various sickness and diseases. Corporal Thomas Robinson, in the prime of his life at age 26, died in 1811. Private John Nicholson, really only a child at 16 years old, died in 1810. The inscription on his headstone is heartbreaking, seemingly a message to a grieving mother:

> *The fairest flower that nature shows*
> *Sustains the sharpest doom;*
> *His life was like the morning rose*
> *That withers in its bloom.*
> *Weep not, Mother, for John is at rest;*
> *His sins forgot and in heaven blest.*

Sickness certainly claimed its share of soldiers, but the post surgeon's grimmest work would have begun once war was declared in the summer of 1812. Dozens of wounded soldiers, their limbs shattered by cannon balls or with musket balls buried deep within their flesh, were pulled from the battlefield of Queenston Heights that October and raced to the hospital at Fort George. The chaos would have threatened to overwhelm the surgeon: men screaming in pain, blood streaming onto the floor-boards until they were covered with crimson pools and slippery underfoot, bloodied rags and uniforms tossed about, the stench of burnt flesh. It would have been hell-ish, a place of misery and suffering. Many of the men would die in the coming hours and days, despite the sur-geon's best efforts. Imagine the pain they endured in their final moments on this earth. Imagine also the nightmares filled with carnage and the faces of those he could not save that undoubtedly plagued the doctor's dreams for the rest of his days.

These traumatic events stained the ground upon which the hospital stood and are said to have sparked off the hauntings that afflicted the current building when it was built in 1940. For decades, the wood-frame structure served as the residence of the Fort George caretaker. It was during this period, the story goes, that the spirit or spirits first began to make their presence felt. Although the first grounds manager and his family lived in the fort for many years without incident, the same cannot be said of his replacement. After only two years the new care-taker and his wife moved out of their home in Fort George. Items that disappeared and reappeared at ran-dom, as well as unusual noises and strange lights that plagued them at all hours, had both of them on the verge of nervous collapse. They had no choice but to leave, driven out by spirits that for some unknown reason resented their presence.

The strange events continued even after the home was transformed into a gift shop. Many tourists left the building bewildered and unnerved by a variety of paranormal activities.

A few years ago, a female visitor went to use the bathroom located within the gift shop building. While there, she was startled to hear the distinct sound of footsteps treading across the floor directly above her. She thought maybe she was hearing things because the building had no second floor. When the woman began to hear it again—*thump, thump, thump*—she fled from the building to the man waiting patiently outside for her. Her heart pounded in her chest. After catching her breath and composing herself, she shared what she had just experienced. Naturally dubious but also somewhat curious, the man followed her back into the bathroom. Sure enough, after entering the facilities they both distinctly heard the sound of heavy footsteps pacing back and forth on the floor above.

Thinking they were the butt of a practical joke, the two of them ran outside and circled the building, hoping to catch the prankster in the act or to find any explanation for the noises they both heard. But even after circling the building several times they found no one, nothing that could possibly explain the footsteps. There was no sign of a person, or an animal for that matter, that might have been responsible. The couple were reluctantly forced to the conclusion that the sounds they heard were not of this life. In their hearts they both knew they had heard spectral footsteps from someone long dead.

A possible explanation emerges if one digs a bit into the history of the building. A painting of the fort made by a military surgeon stationed in Niagara just before the

War of 1812 depicts the hospital building having a second floor. Could it be that an entity from long ago haunts the upper floor, trudging across floorboards that haven't existed for 200 years?

Fort George plays host to lantern-lit ghost tours throughout the operating season. During one such ghost tour in the summer of 2002, a woman named Wendy happened to look up toward the gift shop. Near the back of the building, on the side wall, she saw a rectangular doorway blazing with orange light. It looked almost as though the building was on fire, so the woman breathed a sigh of relief when the light faded moments later; at least the building wasn't about to burn down before her eyes. But relief was soon replaced by disbelief. What had caused the light? One of the security guards on duty that night had witnessed the unusual glow as well and had no explanation. The gift shop was closed for the evening and locked up tight, so no one could have been inside to turn on a light. It was a mystery.

The spirit who lurks within the former gift shop only rarely makes himself visible, and then he appears only for brief moments before melting away in front of speechless visitors. A participant in one of the 2007 Fort George ghost tours had a startling encounter with this shy ghost. He felt an ominous sensation come over him as the group approached the gift shop. The feeling only grew more intense as they drew near, as if the feeling of dread radiated out from the wooden building, and a shudder rippled along his shoulders. The man felt oddly compelled to peer into the window. His face was pressed up against the glass when his breath suddenly locked in his throat—staring back at him was a shadowy face with black, beady eyes squinted to mere slits. Their eyes locked for a moment, and then the sinister face faded into the depths of the darkened interior.

In August 1996, a new guide followed along on one of the ghost tours for training purposes. As he walked alongside the crowd he looked in the direction of the gift shop and was bewildered to see an almost transparent man standing just behind the building. In the evening gloom it took a few moments for his vision to focus, and as it did horror began to overcome him—the apparition was wearing a white smock covered in blood. As the young guide inched closer to the building, he could see that the luminous figure was also carrying a bucket of what seemed to be severed human limbs. The figure disappeared in the blink of an eye.

Later that year, more and more reports came in from ghost tour participants who reported sightings of the same man, dressed in white and standing near the gift shop. No one really knows who this spirit is, but those who have witnessed the apparition believe that he was a surgeon at the fort long ago, perhaps a man to whom fell the grim task of amputating shattered limbs in the aftermath of the Battle of Queenston Heights when the Fort George hospital was overflowing with grievously wounded soldiers.

"One night, custodial staff cleaning after the fort closed up noticed that the light had been left on in the basement…not a terribly uncommon thing as the area is used for gift store storage," says Kyle Upton, who runs Ghosts Tours of Niagara, the popular tour group that leads tourists on a lantern-lit exploration of the fort's haunted heritage. "But then she noticed a man moving around downstairs. This was more unexpected, as she knew the Friends of Fort George staff (who operate the gift store) had left. She rushed to the staff building and came back with another employee who had been working late, but no sign of the man could be found. All basement windows were secure and intact, the gift shop locked and alarmed."

Lights are known to turn on and off in the basement, as if a ghostly hand is playing with the switch. Similarly, the motion activated lights in the new bathroom flare to life at night despite the fact that the building is empty and locked. In addition, mysterious figures are sometimes seen through windows moving around inside the building at all hours. When staff race to confront the intruder, they invariably find no one. It's as if the figure simply fades away into nothingness.

Perhaps the most chilling of accounts occurred a few years ago when a female psychic named Abby, along with two companions, visited the site in hopes of experiencing some form of paranormal activity. They decided that a daylight investigation was just as likely to result in an encounter with the supernatural as one at night, and by coming during the day they would be free of the crowds that gather in the dark for the famous lantern-lit tours. They anticipated that the stone powder magazine or perhaps the damp and coldly sinister subterranean tunnel would be the most likely places to have a bone-chilling brush with the dead. But despite how spooky those locations seemed, none of the three investigators experienced anything out of the ordinary there, nor did anything happen in either the barracks or the officers' quarters. With their hopes dimming, they turned to the gift shop.

Having heard that some people see a ghostly figure floating about the building and its surroundings, they paused outside and lingered along one of the walls. Abby placed her hands against the wooden boards, feeling their grain and trying to reach out to any spirit residing within. Sure enough, a cool sensation numbed the tips of her fingers, spread to the palms of her hands and then crept up her arms to seep through her whole body. This was a familiar feeling to her. It meant she had made contact with the deceased.

"We know you are here. People have heard you and seen you. I can sense you. We know that you are here. Can you give us a sign?" she said gently, trying to coax the spirit out of hiding. When nothing happened after a few long moments of silence she tried again. "Please give us a sign. Bang on the wall."

"I don't have to!" said a thin, grating voice.

All three investigators nearly jumped out of their skin. The words had come out of thin air. It was a distinctly male voice, laced in malice and clearly adamant that it wasn't about to cooperate with the investigation. The spot then got really cold, cold enough to cause flesh to goose bump on a warm summer day. Abby, still connected to the wall, felt the supernatural chill particularly strongly. A gnawing cold seeped out of the wood, crawling its way painfully up her arms, causing her to grimace in agony. This was a frightening sensation she had never before experienced. Reflexively she jerked her hands away to break contact, and as soon as she did all three friends noticed the temperature begin to climb so that within moments the area was warm again.

The ghosts of Fort George's former hospital died in situations that evoked extreme emotion, and, as these three paranormal investigators found out in startling fashion, these emotions have only grown more powerful and intense beyond the grave. As a result, a visit to this important historical site and popular tourist attraction never fails to evoke a response in visitors. Sometimes it's just an appreciation of the past or the hardships endured by soldiers posted here. Other times, however, the response is far more chilling and personal, a reaction to a creepy supernatural encounter with spirits from the past that remain bound to the present.

Fort George played an important role during the traumatic War of 1812, and a lot of blood and tears were shed within its walls. It's no wonder that restless spirits quietly whisper of troubled times long past.

Officers' Quarters

Moonlight shone white on the rooftops of the buildings enclosed within the walls of Fort George. Never before had Taylor seen moonlight so misty clear, so eerie. The grounds through which the ghost tour passed seemed unreal, enchanted. When Taylor and her husband arrived in the evening gloom to participate in the walk, she told him that she wasn't afraid. But no sooner had they entered the first building and the guide begun to tell of spirits that return from beyond the grave than she began to feel the cold hands of fear gripping her. She found herself imagining horrifying undead crawling from their coffins to stalk the night. It took no little courage for her to step foot into the various darkened buildings to which the tour guide led his followers.

Toward the end of the evening, the lantern-carrying guide directed the group into the Officers' Quarters. For long seconds Taylor resisted. She was rooted to the spot just outside the door. Something about the building disturbed her. Finally, with the gentle reassurance of her husband's hand resting on her arm, she reluctantly entered. Inside, dark shadows stretched out from fine furniture, the lantern's light reflected eerily off glassware set out on a table ready for a night's entertaining, and the curtains on the canopy bed seemed to flutter despite the lack of breeze.

That's when she saw it. The blanket on the bed, so flawlessly smooth and tight a moment ago, suddenly sank down and formed a depression. The shape moulded into the blanket was vaguely man-shaped, as if someone had just lain down to sleep. Taylor stammered as she tried to point out the bed to her husband. Then her eyes went wide with fright and a lump formed in her throat, cutting off her words entirely. A faint figure, that of a youthful-looking man, suddenly materialized on the bed. His eyes were closed and he seemed at rest, peaceful. From the floor around the bed rose wispy headstones. They were tilted at all angles, like crooked teeth. Taylor stepped back, retreating from the frightful scene. Her hands went to her throat as she tried desperately to scream, but her voice was paralyzed with terror. She knew it had been a bad idea to enter the Officers' Quarters that night...

The Officers' Quarters is the most distinctive building within Fort George. It sits at the centre of the fort, facing the gate across the parade ground. Unlike the other buildings in the fort, which are finished with a dull blue-grey paint that feels cold and dreary, or even left with the large square-hewn timbers exposed, this building is painted a warm and welcoming bright yellow. The Officers' Quarters has more windows than other buildings have, allowing sunlight to stream in to make the rooms feel airy and alive. Fruit trees grow on the grounds alongside the building, and the entire compound is encircled by a white picket fence. It's obvious to even the untrained eye that men of importance resided here.

Because senior officers assigned to Fort George would have been able to afford their own apartments or homes in the town of Niagara-on-the-Lake, only the younger ensigns, lieutenants and captains would have resided at the fort. These junior officers were required to remain on base around the clock to oversee the training, discipline and administration of the fort and its soldiers. After all, a senior officer couldn't be expected to leave the warmth of his bed in the middle of the night to ensure sentries were posted, or to wake in the pre-dawn gloom to oversee the daily roll-call as soldiers gathered on the parade ground. Instead, the mundane tasks were left to the younger, less experienced officers.

Junior officers were privileged young men from wealthy families with social status, and their accommodations were quite luxurious in keeping with the standards to which they were used. Inside, in spite of the spartan furnishings found in the enlisted men's barracks, you find plush feather beds, fine furniture and luxuries the average soldier could only dream of. The best food and plenty of expensive alcohol would have been served, and cigar smoke would have hung heavily in the air. The atmosphere of the place would have been more akin to a gentlemen's social club than a military post, with the officers spending much of their time playing the pianoforte, gambling and gaming, reading fine literature and hosting parties where they danced with young ladies of the community under the watchful eyes of their escorts. Before war came to ruin things, a posting at Fort George was a plum one for young officers sent to serve in Canada.

It's been more than 150 years since British soldiers have lived in Fort George, and yet not all of them have given up residence. Cut down in battle with the balance of their lives still ahead of them, one or more young officers returned to the Officers' Quarters to haunt its luxurious rooms. Can you blame lost souls for returning to a place of such refinement? Why lurk upon the forlorn battlefield where you fell when you can enjoy a far more cheerful atmosphere here? Why continue to lie in a rotting coffin when you can rest in comfort in a plush bed? Given the choice, the ghostly officers made their way back to the last place they called home, the Officers' Quarters at Fort George.

Apparitions and bizarre phenomena are frequently reported within the building. Voices whisper in ears, spectral hands shove the living, candles are blown out and flashlights mysteriously die, an ethereal cat jumps off furniture to hide under a couch or table, visitors are inexplicably brought to tears, and the pianoforte plays music by itself. Long-dead officers are seen, going about the routines of their previous lives as if unaware they are being watched by startled onlookers. Sometimes these men are wispy figures, transparent and foggy, while at other times they seem as much flesh and blood as you and I. A large proportion of these experiences occurs in October, particularly in the days leading up to Halloween.

Halloween is known as the witching season, a time when we fall under a spell that causes our imaginations to run wild. Autumn has arrived, and night descends earlier than it does over the preceding summer months. The air has cooled. Trees are barren, their fallen leaves rustling underfoot and racing across the ground as if fleeing some unseen horror lurking in the dark. The darkness of the night is often accompanied by cold mists and fog, thin tendrils of which reach out like ghostly hands. At this time of year, it's easy to imagine that every sound heard in the blackness is a predatory monster stalking you, and that the corpses of the dead might rise to sweep away the living in a tide of decay. It's perhaps little wonder that so many people claim to have supernatural experiences during this season; we're subconsciously geared up for it.

But this predisposition isn't enough to explain away the rash of paranormal phenomena that has taken place within the Officers' Quarters on Halloween. Respected staff and visitors alike have breathlessly reported that things just aren't right in the building come October, and the weird events seem to build toward a crescendo at All Hallows Eve.

The guided ghost tour of Halloween night, 1997, began innocently enough. The participating group was an eager blend of young and old, men and women, skeptics and those certain of the existence of ghosts. Every one of them undoubtedly privately wanted to see disembodied undead soldiers marching across the Common or standing at attention in one of the buildings. Be careful what you wish for.

While the group was passing through the Officers' Quarters, an elderly man suddenly grew quite upset by something he saw. His face drained of colour and he was visibly rattled. When asked what was wrong, he pointed a shaky finger toward a table in the sitting room. There, he said through trembling lips, he had seen two soldiers. They were dressed in the distinctive red uniforms of the 19th-century British army, with large black hats, the mark of officers, sitting atop the table. One of these men sat in a chair, leaning intently over the table as he studied curled maps and assorted papers. He seemed absorbed in his work, occasionally taking notes with a feather quill. The other, younger man stood behind the first man and peered over his shoulder at the maps and papers. The elderly tour member thought for a second that they were re-enactors but realized his mistake when they disappeared within the blink of an eye. Were these British soldiers still performing staff work or planning a campaign in a war that has been over for 200 years? Maybe one was the hero of Queenston Heights, General Brock himself?

The spirits residing within the Officers' Quarters made themselves known the following Halloween as well.

Poltergeist activity is a relatively common occurrence in the building. Items move about as if by unseen hands frequently enough that veteran staff members of the fort and ghost tours are almost casual about it. But for newer employees and visitors, seeing a door unlatch by itself or a drape being brushed aside by an invisible hand can be terribly frightening. And so it was during the Halloween tour of 1998, when a ghost tour staff member insisted on being reassigned to another position halfway through the evening just to get away from whatever lurked within the building. An invisible presence had methodically worn down his courage over the period of a few hours, manipulating items in a sanity-testing campaign intended to chase away an unwelcome visitor.

According to Kyle Upton, who operates Ghost Tours of Niagara and has written a pair of books about paranormal activity at the fort (*Niagara Ghosts* volumes I and II), this employee was a dedicated young man who wasn't the least bit skittish, nor did he have an overactive imagination. Not once had he complained about his assigned tasks or reported experiencing anything supernatural, so his behaviour this particular evening was all the more unsettling.

On Halloween night, the young man was given the job of providing security for the Officers' Quarters. Essentially, it was his task to ensure none of the items inside were stolen or vandalized, and to prevent the public from entering without their guides being present. During the time tour groups were in the building listening to eerie tales of the macabre, he was to provide illumination for the rear of the group so that people didn't walk into walls or trip over furnishings. There were long lulls between the arrival of the tours, which meant the young man was alone in the building for lonely stretches with only a candle's flickering flame for company and lighting.

During one such lull, the employee heard the sound of footsteps shuffling through the halls. Thinking perhaps it was a straying member of one of the tour groups, he went to investigate. With only the flame of this candle and the moonlight filtering through windows, the young man made his way through the building, searching the shadows and calling out to whoever may have ventured into the building. Though several times the footsteps sounded nearby, as if coming from the next room, the man found no one. From room to room, the very emptiness of the Officers' Quarters caused his heart to beat faster, banging like a drum in his chest. There was no doubting the distinctive sound of footsteps, and yet there was no one to have made them. That left only one explanation. The staff member swallowed hard; he of course had heard about the ghosts inhabiting the Officers' Quarters, but actually encountering one was far more unnerving than he had expected.

With nothing to be done about a ghostly intruder, the young man went back to his original post to await the arrival of the upcoming tour group. He continued to hear shuffling footsteps through the halls but willed himself to pay no attention to them. When it failed to get a response, the ghost took its mischief to a new level by blowing out the man's candle to cast him into darkness. Fumbling for matches with shaky fingers, the young man had no sooner got the candle relit than it mysteriously blew out again. He struck another match, and in the quivering flame thought he caught momentary sight of a shadowy figure in the room with him. His throat was suddenly parched and dry as fear began to take hold.

Then the doors in the building started to open and close on their own. Each time a hinge creaked, a new shiver ran down his spine. Finally, after what seemed like hours of torture but was likely only a few minutes, his courage failed him. The young man ran outside, preferring to await the tour in the cold rather than remain another minute in that building when it was clear to him that his presence was not welcome. When the tour finally arrived the terror was still too raw and he refused to enter, demanding a new assignment somewhere—anywhere—else. He swore then that he would never again risk the interior of the Officers' Quarters alone at night, and he lived up to that promise.

Sonja is a longtime employee of Fort George who also refuses to step so much as a foot into the Officers' Quarters after dark, fearful of what lurks within the building's void-like darkness. Her wariness is the result of the terrifying events of one night in particular, a night that she can't forget no matter how hard she tries. When Fort George closed its doors to the tourist crowd at the end of that day it was Sonja's turn to lock up the Officers' Quarters and set the building's alarm. Before she could do so, she had to sweep through the building to ensure no one was being locked inside. This particular day, for no reason she could explain, Sonja searched the building twice because of an unsettling feeling that there was someone in the building with her. It gnawed at her, so she went from room to room, peering into each one in turn, always with the tingling sensation that unseen eyes were following her every move. She found no one, however, so she finally concluded her imagination was playing tricks on her and locked up.

Only a few hours later, Sonja returned to the fort to prepare for the night's ghost tour. She found the Officers' Quarters exactly as she had left it earlier. Lighting a candle, she noted the same uncomfortable atmosphere within. Something set her hair on end and caused her skin to goose pimple. She didn't linger long. She left the building and put the sense of creeping malice behind her.

Later that evening the ghost tour approached the Officers' Quarters, its members unaware of the unsettling feeling that had chased Sonja away. The tour guide urged his excited followers to huddle around the window looking into the sitting room, and he began to relate some of the many paranormal events that people have witnessed in the building over the years. As the guide was talking, members of the group took turns pressing their noses to the glass to peer into the room's shadow-filled interior, illuminated only by the candles Sonja had lit earlier that evening. Suddenly, six people gasped and quickly stepped back from the window, their faces ashen and their eyes wide with fright. All of them had seen the door to the junior officers' wing swing shut on its own. When they told the tour guide what they'd seen, he had no explanation. The door is heavy and the hinges stiff, requiring considerable effort to push it closed. A breeze, even if there had been one sweeping into the building, could not possibly have been responsible, and there was no other earthly explanation. Members of the group were still excitedly talking about the experience as the guide led them away from the building and toward the front gate to end the evening's event.

Hoping to get a head start on locking up so she could get home early, Sonja entered the Officers' Quarters to blow out the candles just as soon as the tour had moved away. She gazed in silent astonishment at the sight of the closed door leading to the junior officers' wing. It had been open hours before, and now it wasn't. She was holding the only keys to the building, so how then had that door closed? She couldn't explain it, which only added to the unease that had settled over her earlier in the day while in the building. Unnerved, Sonja blew out the candles and quickly fled the building, activating the alarm and locking the door as she went.

Sonja wanted nothing more than to race from Fort George to the solace of her home, so her heart sank when she saw the tour group lingering near the front gate, still deep in conversation. She didn't want to panic the public by racing past them in terror—how would that look, she thought to herself—so reluctantly she remained just outside the Officers' Quarters. Trapped in the courtyard behind the building, too close for comfort to whatever lurked inside, things only got worse.

From within the locked and alarmed Officers' Quarters, Sonja heard the antique pianoforte begin to play. The ghostly fingers dancing across the keys were those of a talented player who performed a flawless rendition of Beethoven's "Moonlight Sonata," composed in 1801. The music increased in volume as the song reached its climax.

When the song was finished, the music died away and silence once again fell over the building. Blessedly, Sonja saw the tour group dissolving. She ran for the front gate, putting the Officers' Quarters and its ethereal denizen behind her. The night's events were so traumatic that she promised never again to lock up the Officers' Quarters by herself, a promise she has faithfully kept.

One of the more common phenomena of the Officers' Quarters sees staff enter in the morning to find the blanket and mattress of a particular canopy-draped bed with a man-shaped indentation in the middle of it, as if someone had been sleeping on it. The staff member will tighten the springs, fluff the bolster, turn over the mattress and tuck in and smooth the sheets and blankets. And yet, the following morning the dent has returned.

"The sagging bed is a real mystery because it looks just like someone has been lying on top, although anyone doing so would have been detected on the alarm," says Ron Dale of Parks Canada. The only explanation is that one of the unquiet dead lurking within Fort George has slept upon it. And where better to rest? Would you rather sleep on a hard wooden plank thinly covered by a straw-filled mattress, as found in the common soldiers' barracks, or on a plush, comfortable canopy bed in the Officers' Quarters? The choice is an easy one.

It's interesting to note that whoever sleeps on the bed is tied to the building itself and not the furnishing, since the bed is a reproduction only 30 years old. As a result, it's safe to assume that the mysterious nighttime napper is the unseen spectre of a junior officer who served here two centuries ago, and who was killed in battle during the

War of 1812. It's tragic that an evening's rest, rather than an eternal one, is the best this spirit can hope for.

These varied tales represent just a small sampling of the unusual, sometimes chilling events that have occurred in the Officers' Quarters over the years. It seems that every year new ones emerge, cementing the building's reputation as the most haunted location within the walls of historic Fort George. Its warmly painted exterior and luxurious furnishings are deceiving: the Officers' Quarters looks inviting and comfortable, and yet many people find themselves chased away by forlorn spirits.

While most of the junior officers who resided in the building have made the transition to the other side with ease, the ghosts of one or two young men remain confused and lost. They were almost certainly killed in battle. Any regrets they felt as their lifeblood flowed from their bodies have become more powerful and intense beyond the grave, forming manacles that shackle them to a world in which they no longer belong. It takes a brave person to enter the Officers' Quarters at night. Even those who are prepared for the possibility of witnessing supernatural phenomena recoil in fear when faced with the intensity of the haunting. Officers are used to commanding respect, and apparently that doesn't change just because they die.

Laura Secord Homestead

Dusk falls early in November, creating dark shadows like black pools beneath trees even when sunlight still glows a faint red on the horizon. From the back seat of the car, Sabina noted how desolate the scenery became once the light began to fail. Trees, barren of leaves, transformed into twisted skeletal shapes. Woods were suddenly dense and foreboding. The expanse of the Niagara River, so scenic during the day, became a void of darkness. To Sabina, the outskirts of Niagara-on-the-Lake, full of picturesque wineries with manicured rows of grapevines and elegant homes, and just a month earlier full of fall tourists, had become oddly menacing with the onset of evening. Even as the car passed through the village of Queenston, few lights poked through the dark veil that had suddenly descended upon the landscape—streetlights were non-existent, the roads were empty of other cars, and the few lights peeking out from homes seemed distant and feeble.

Suddenly, a pale blue light caught everyone's attention. Matt, the driver, instinctively slowed the car. All eyes turned toward the eerie glow, which seemed to wrap the Laura Secord Homestead with ethereal illumination. They all saw it at the same time: a woman in a long dress and hair in an outdated bun, standing in the building's yard. The woman began to move toward the home. She seemed to be floating, so lightly did she move. Sabina's heart was beating so hard she could feel it throbbing in her neck, and when she tried to swallow, her throat refused to cooperate; it was like she was trying to swallow a mouthful of chalk. She watched the faces of her friends and saw that they had gone as white as snow, their eyes wide with disbelief and apprehension. Turning her gaze back to the spectral woman, Sabina watched as she glided up to the door—boarded up for the winter—and simply passed through. If Sabina alone had seen it she might have questioned her sanity, but with two other people witnessing the same haunting scene, only one conclusion was possible: she had seen a ghost.

Sabina and her friends aren't alone in believing the Laura Secord Homestead museum is haunted. Many others, tourists and staff members alike, have been left with the same conviction after experiencing something strange and unexplainable in and around the 200-year-old frame building. Laura Secord was a notably strong-willed woman in life, so perhaps it should come as no surprise that her spirit may defy the conventions of death and remain behind in her home rather than cross over to some other plane of existence. And she may not be the only ghost in residence; eyewitness accounts seem to suggest that she has unwelcome company.

The museum is one of the most popular attractions in the Niagara region. A private residence until the 1960s, the home was purchased by the Laura Secord Candy Company, restored to its early-19th-century appearance and opened as a museum in 1972. When the candy company passed into American hands, the museum was gifted to the Niagara Parks Commission. Guided by costumed staff, guests travel back in time to Laura's era as they explore the heritage house, learn fascinating things about the heroine and the time in which she lived, and interact with other historic personalities including Laura's husband James, their neighbours, and soldiers from both the British and American armies. But one never truly knows whether the historic figure they encounter is a costumed staff member or the spirit of someone long deceased.

The spectral encounters at the Laura Secord Homestead are a mixed bunch. Some are spine-tingling, others merely curious. To understand the paranormal activity within this board-and-batten home, one needs to appreciate the turmoil and tragedies of the Secord family. Blood and tears soaked deep into the building's aged floorboards, staining the wood with powerful emotions that give the home an unusually strong energy to this day. Indeed, many of the reported accounts of spectral activity seem to be echoes of specific events that occurred here 200 years ago.

Although today she is known as a Canadian heroine, Laura Secord was born in the United States. The oldest of four daughters of Thomas and Elizabeth Ingersoll, she was born in Westfield, Massachusetts, on September 13, 1775, just as the American Revolution was beginning. Massachusetts was one of the areas where feeling against the British ran high, so it is hardly surprising that Thomas joined the American patriots. Despite his anti-British leanings, Thomas moved his family to Upper Canada in 1795 to take advantage of the government's offer of free land, and opened a tavern in the Niagara village of Queenston. It was there that Laura met and fell in love with an aspiring merchant named James Secord. The two were married in 1797.

Strange things happen at the Laura Secord Homestead.

For the first few years of her marriage to James Secord, Laura lived a comfortable existence. True, she worked hard, but her husband was a relatively successful business-man and they enjoyed luxuries such as lace, fine china and two male servants. The future looked bright for the Secords and their young family.

That all changed when the War of 1812 erupted and Niagara became a battlefield soaked in blood and hatred. During the war, the Secords and other colonists of the Niagara region lived in a constant state of fear, always worried about their personal safety and the well-being of loved ones, struggling every day to tend crops, care for livestock and conduct business despite the disruptions caused by war. As an American and the daughter of a man who had fought against the British a generation earlier, Laura may well have been viewed with some sus-picion by neighbours who doubted her loyalty.

The fall of 1812 brought the war to the Niagara peninsula with a vengeance. On October 13, in a cold drizzle, the Americans crossed the Niagara River and attacked Queenston Heights, a dominating plateau that overlooked the Secord home. As a member of the militia, James was heavily involved in the fighting that raged back and forth all day, leaving as many as 500 men dead and wounded littered along the Heights' wooded slopes. In the fading October light, word reached Laura that the British had won but that James was missing. She raced to the battlefield and, in the growing darkness, with the pitiful moans of wounded and dying men all around her, began a desperate search for her husband.

When she finally found him he was in agonizing pain and unable to move, shot through the shoulder and knee. With the assistance of a neighbour, Laura had him brought back to their home, which had been looted by American soldiers during the course of the fighting. James spent several feverish nights in bed, crying out in pain whenever the laudanum Laura spoon fed him wore off, his restless sleep interrupted by terrifying dreams of the nightmarish battle he had just endured.

In fact, James' wounds were still slowly healing when the Americans invaded again the following spring, capturing Fort George on May 27 and compelling the British to retreat 30 miles. Niagara was now occupied territory. Laura had already suffered as a result of the conflict and so tried to remain aloof from it and the enemy soldiers who marched through her village. Within the walls of her home at least, Laura felt secure and apart from the surrounding chaos; her home was her haven and her solitude.

You can imagine then the fear Laura felt when a small group of American troops appeared on her doorstep on June 21, 1813, demanding food and shelter for the night. Laura reluctantly agreed and allowed the men into her home. What choice did she have?

During the course of the meal, Laura overheard the soldiers talking in hushed voices of their army's plan to surprise the unsuspecting British forces at Beaver Dams in the coming days. It was to be a trap. Laura kept a straight face, pretending not to have heard while she went about serving food to her unwelcome guests, but inside she was in turmoil. She was horrified at the potential consequences of an American victory in the coming battle; the war could drag on for years more, and enemy occupation of Niagara might become permanent.

The Secords realized how important it was to warn the British of the upcoming attack, but who would take the message? James certainly couldn't go; he had yet to fully recover from injuries suffered the year before. The responsibility fell to Laura. But was she up to the task? After her husband had been wounded and her home invaded by the American soldiers she felt vulnerable and violated. What could she, a woman, do to defend her country when she couldn't even defend her family? The weight of the burden bore heavily on her shoulders and she struggled with deciding what to do with the information. Laura knew in her heart it was up to her to venture out into the midst of all the fighting and warn the British of the horrifying plans she had overheard.

At 4:30 the next morning, well before the sun had risen above the horizon, she set out. It had rained hard during the night so the ground was a mire of mud, and even at this early hour the country steamed with humidity. It promised to be a stifling day. But Laura was on a desperate mission and wasn't about to let anything—or anyone—stand in her way. To minimize the chance of meeting an American patrol, she took roundabout routes and avoided the main roads between villages. Doing so added hours to her walk, and each hour added fresh misery. The terrain was rough, covered in high grasses and brush, and the heat was so oppressive it wasn't long before her clothing was soaked with sweat. Her feet ached and blistered. Her eyes blurred from the heat, the humidity and the fatigue. Still, she kept moving. Alone and hungry, she summoned all her strength to complete her vital mission.

As the sun set there was some relief from the heat, but there were still other hazards to contend with: clouds of mosquitoes, night-prowling animals and the very real chance that in the darkness she might lose her way or become disoriented and break a limb tumbling into a ravine or over a fallen tree. At one point she even lost her shoes; her feet were raw and bleeding, so tender that each step was agony. Finally, when her strength had been all but sapped, and having walked more than 20 miles, Laura saw in the distance the glow from campfires. Feeling a sense of relief that her ordeal might soon be at an end, she stumbled toward the lights.

Relief changed to trepidation when she realized the fires were those of a Native camp. Laura had been raised on stories of blood-thirsty Indians who scalped white men and tortured their women, and she was naturally afraid. Should she go forward and approach the Natives?

Fear and sense of duty fought an internal tug-of-war. But with her strength all but gone, Laura realized she really didn't have a choice. If she was to warn the British she would have to put aside her concerns, enter the camp and convince these warriors to let her pass.

The Indians were shocked to see a dishevelled white woman stumbling from the forest, and while they listened to her story they were skeptical. The epic journey she described seemed impossible for a woman to have accomplished, and some of them wondered whether it was an American ruse. But when Laura explained the urgency of her mission the Natives relented and took her across the fields to the headquarters of Lieutenant James FitzGibbons, commander of the British forces in the area.

The young officer was shocked at her condition: "Mrs. Secord was a person of slight and delicate frame, and made the effort in weather excessively warm, and I dreaded at the time that she must suffer in health in consequence of fatigue and anxiety, she having been exposed to danger from the enemy, through whose line of communication she had to pass," he would later write. But the news she brought justified her exertions. It was potentially war-changing, and FitzGibbons knew it. Armed with foreknowledge of American intentions, he was able to ambush and soundly defeat the American army at the ensuing Battle of Beaver Dams on June 23.

But Laura received no recognition for her role in the victory, nor any form of financial reward. In fact, the Secord family's fortunes never really recovered from the disruption brought about by the war and they struggled most years thereafter. Laura's financial woes only got worse when on February 22, 1841, James died and left her a widow at age 64. It was only in 1861 that Laura, by then an elderly woman with steel-grey hair and pale eyes, received a measure of the credit that was she long deserved. That year, Albert Edward, Prince of Wales and Queen Victoria's eldest son, was touring Canada and stopped in Queenston to pay tribute to veterans of the War of 1812. After being told of Laura's heroic adventure, he made note that upon his return to England he would arrange a reward for her. He was true to his word. The prince sent £100 as thanks for her bravery. It was to be the only financial compensation Laura Secord ever received for risking life and limb on behalf of her adopted country.

Many people believe the spirit of Laura Secord continues to watch over her home.

Laura's travels came to end in 1868 at the age of 93. Upon her death, she was laid to rest alongside her husband in Drummond Hill Cemetery, Niagara Falls. More than a century later their Queenston home was opened as a tourist destination. Every year, thousands of visitors enjoy a guided tour of the home in which Laura and her husband spent the greater part of their adult lives. They learn about life in the early 19th century, the turbulent times in which they lived, the nature of Laura's bravery and how she was ultimately elevated into a position among Canada's great heroes.

Some tourists leave the Laura Secord Homestead with a particularly powerful appreciation for the woman and her life. Laura may have lived her last years in Chippawa, but her spirit, many believe, returned to her beloved Queenston home and continues to dwell on the premises to this day. Strange goings-on in the house over the past four decades seem to add credence to this belief. People have reported hearing voices on the second floor; not the distinct voices of staff or visitors, but otherworldly whisperings that hang in the air like a quiet breeze. People look around, but there's no one there.

Others have reported seeing a female ghost in one of the upstairs bedrooms, standing motionless at the foot of the bed, her lifeless gaze never straying from the bed. Is this Laura tending to James as he recovered from the injuries sustained at the Battle of Queenston Heights? One time, this ghostly manifestation was accompanied by the pitiful moans of man in obvious pain.

One visitor was particularly startled by Laura's sudden appearance. Recently retired, Phil and his wife decided to visit the Laura Secord Homestead for the first time. Joining a small group of fellow tourists, they were led through the building by a costumed guide who shared the life story of this Canadian heroine and the brave deeds that made her a legend. Phil passed a large mirror hanging on a plaster wall. In its dim depths he saw the reflection of someone behind him—a woman in a long but plain dress. She and the clothing she wore looked old-fashioned, something out of the 19th century. Phil assumed another guide had stealthily joined the group from behind. He turned to face her, but there was no one there.

His heart flattened in his chest. He had seen someone in the mirror. He knew he had. His wife caught the confusion in his eyes and the sudden draining of colour from his cheeks. "What's wrong dear? You look like…"

Phil shot his wife a long, hard look. She took the hint and gave him some privacy, wandering away to listen as the guide shared another historical anecdote. It took a few moments for the man to reconcile with the fact that he had seen a ghost, and that the ghost was probably that of Laura Secord. But what shocked him the most was that he wasn't terrified. Sure he was stunned, perhaps a little scared, but he was also exhilarated by the experience. He even has theory: he believes Laura Secord joined the tour group, trailing unseen behind, out of curiosity about the unannounced guests in her home.

Another time, the sounds of breaking furniture and smashing crockery were heard from the kitchen. The noises were loud and violent, as if someone was trashing the home. But when they were investigated, the floor was not littered with splintered wood and fragments of pitchers and bowls as expected. Instead the room was orderly and tranquil. As we'll remember, the Secord home had been ransacked once, but that was almost 200 years earlier. No doubt the experience of having enemies invade the privacy of her home, steal personal items and vandalize the property deeply traumatized Laura. Were the otherworldly sounds experienced by the modern-day visitor a type of echo from this event two centuries prior, perhaps imprinted upon the building by Laura's feelings of violation? It certainly seems possible.

Sheila's experience at the museum was less dramatic than most and certainly didn't cause her sleepless nights afterward, but it was no less emotionally powerful: "I recall the first time I walked into Laura Secord's home, which now is a museum for all to enjoy. After walking through the door I stood in the foyer, waited graciously for Mrs. Secord to greet me herself, materializing out of thin air to welcome me into her home and perhaps offer me a cup of tea. But of course that did not happen. And yet, her presence was definitely with me as I walked through her home. I swore I could feel a gentle hand on my arm, as if guiding me about, and occasionally I would brush up against someone who wasn't there. Mrs. Secord showed real spirit trying to protect her country and her house, and it is so fitting that she still watches over the home even a century or so later. Her strength and will to survive are still deep within its walls. I instantly felt her presence around me, kind, brave, loving in a motherly way, but most important a woman who would have done everything to protect her home and family. One cannot go and experience the home of Laura Secord and not feel touched by the bravery of this woman. I know I did and I still feel that she was an example that women should follow—there is nothing that we can't do if we put our heart and soul to it."

Of course, guests aren't the only ones to have brushes with the supernatural here. Employees of the Niagara Parks Commission spend more time than anyone within the historic building, so it stands to reason they would occasionally encounter something unusual. "Beth" (whose name has been changed at her request) worked for Niagara Parks some years ago, spending most of her time at the Laura Secord Homestead, where she felt strangely at home. Beth was always the quickest to say there was no such thing as ghosts, but one summer at the museum radically altered her view. Her first experience occurred early in the morning, well before tourists began to arrive for the day. The building was silent and dim, the summer sun not yet beating through the windows to chase away the shadows. No sooner had Beth passed through the door than a strange feeling began to come over her. Her hair bristled, a cold chill seeped its way through her body, and goose bumps crawled over her flesh. Instinctively she knew she was not alone. The now-frightened young woman could feel someone's presence, yet she could see no one.

"I called out, but got no answer," Beth explains. "I thought maybe my mind was playing tricks on me as I tried to make sense of what I felt. I started to shake off my fear, at least enough to be able to move again. Slowly, I started to walk farther into the home. But no sooner did I begin than I froze to a stop, as I clearly heard footsteps across the room above me." Terror gripped Beth like a boney hand and wouldn't let go, paralyzing her. Her eyes widened with disbelief as a white figure wearing an old-fashioned dress gently floated in front of her. Seconds later, the spectral woman slowly faded from sight.

"After that first incident I continued to occasionally hear strange noises in the house, even though there was never anyone in the building. Sometimes it gave me the chills as I entered the home, but I was never afraid again. I knew whoever this ghost was, she didn't mean any harm." If pressed, Beth admits to believing the apparition she saw was Laura Secord herself, making her presence known, perhaps serving a reminder that she is the woman of the house.

The current manager/curator at the Laura Secord Homestead is Melissa Bottomley. She doesn't disbelieve in ghosts, but neither can she honestly say she's had any ghostly encounters at the homestead. "Unfortunately, or very fortunately as I look at it, in my eight years here I have not experienced anything, nor has anyone on my tours. There are usually one or two guests [out of thousands] a year that say they get the heeby-jeebys from the parents' room, but that's about it."

A few Octobers ago a paranormal research group came to investigate the Laura Secord Homestead and its tradition of hauntings. Melissa explains that during their nighttime vigil they captured on audio-tape what sounded like someone walking across the aged floorboards, which naturally excited the group. It wasn't one or two steps, but the distinct sound of someone crossing a room. The level-headed curator accepts that what they recorded may well have been the spectral footsteps of a past resident—she's not a skeptic after all—but also notes that the house is small and every sound echoes. She's uncertain what to make of it all, but is open-minded enough to consider having another paranormal team or a medium come in for further investigation.

Melissa is left wondering, does Laura Secord still inhabit her one-time home as so many people believe? Is it possible that she wanders the rooms of the museum to this very day, bound to them by the eternal connection between herself and the home in which she spent so many years of her life? It was here, after all, that several of her children were born, where she watched helplessly as her 18-year-old daughter succumbed to illness, and where she nursed her husband's war wounds. This home definitely held many emotionally charged memories for Laura, so it's easy to see why her ghost might cling to the home like supernatural mortar. If any woman is strong-willed enough to resist the call of death it is Laura Secord, the simple housewife who through sheer strength of will completed an epic walk to warn the British of an American attack and who perhaps saved Canada.

White House Ghosts

The White House is not only the most famous house in America, but it might be the nation's most haunted house as well. Almost from the time it was built in 1792, stories of ghostly residents have circulated and have only grown more numerous in the centuries since. This is perhaps to be expected. Many people believe that ghosts are a form of psychic energy that remains in a building long after a person's death. Most presidents—and indeed many first ladies—have been powerful personalities in life and might choose to revisit the scenes of their greatest triumphs and tragedies. Indeed, if the stories are to be believed, many American presidents have seen their terms of office extended into the afterlife. But it's not just those who occupied the Oval Office who haunt the seat of American power: politicians and statesmen, one-time staff members and a variety of other figures are said to occupy one or more of the White House's 127 rooms.

In this chapter, we concern ourselves with three spectres tied to the War of 1812: a torch-bearing British soldier whose face glows in the orange flames with sinister intent; President James Madison, the architect of a misguided war who seems to grieve for his sullied reputation; and his first lady, Dolley Madison, a woman beloved in life who has grown legendary in death.

Redcoat Apparition

The British sergeant marched in silence, listening to his men chatter. He was in a foul mood, thinking back on the past two years of war. *Bloody Yanks*, he thought darkly to himself. While the King's army had been preoccupied with fighting Napoleon in Europe, the Americans had sought to stab the British in the back by stealing Canada from the Empire. It was only by the grace of God and the heroic service of Canadian militia and a handful of British soldiers that the Americans had not succeeded. But now, in the summer of 1814, things were different. A tight smile spread across the sergeant's weathered face. The tide had turned. With Napoleon defeated, thousands of battle-hardened troops could be spared for service in North America, and finally the war was coming to the Americans' backyard. *We'll teach these colonials a lesson they won't soon forget*, the sergeant silently vowed.

A few weeks ago, in early August, he and thousands of other British soldiers had landed in Maryland. Almost all of them were battle-hardened veterans of the Peninsular War, having fought in numerous grim battles against the French in Portugal and Spain. Some of the men were criminals, avoiding justice by enlisting, and almost all of them were from the lowest dregs of society, but they were good men and excellent soldiers and the sergeant was proud of them.

His pride had grown with their performance that morning at Bladensburg. There, the British march had been blocked by an American force of 6000, composed of militia, sailors and some regular regiments. In the distance, the spires of the American capital, the target of the British expedition, could be clearly seen. There were only 2600 Redcoats lined up against the Americans and yet, despite being outnumbered two to one, they had easily won the day. Indeed, the sergeant had been surprised, shocked, at how quickly the enemy turned tail to run even with the fate of Washington, D.C. in the balance.

Now, on the afternoon of August 24, as the sergeant and his men marched along a dusty road through the Maryland countryside, nothing stood between them and the American capital. The cavalry rode ahead, searching the landscape for signs of the enemy, but the American army had turned into a panicked mob after Bladensburg, abandoning the capital and its people to the British. There were even rumours that President James Madison had fled faster than his retreating army, in his haste leaving his wife and staff behind at the White House. The grizzled veteran had snickered at that. Soon, he was confident, the army would enter Washington and for the first time in weeks he and his fellow soldiers would sleep in real beds. He looked forward to delivering that humiliation. The thought had just entered his mind when the army erupted in cheers. Ahead in the distance lay the sprawling expanse of the capital city. To a man, the soldiers of the marching British army were excited to be taking the war to the Americans and to be a part of this historic moment. When they were old and grey, huddled by the fire for warmth, they would be able to proudly claim they had participated in the capture of the American capital. They grinned at their general, sitting atop his horse, as he watched them march by on the road.

Washington fell without a shot being fired, and the sergeant was pleased that there were no reports of his soldiers looting or abusing the citizenry. There were rules to war, after all. But while the population was not to be harmed, that protection didn't extend to government property. Earlier in the war the Americans had, in the words of the British Prime Minister, Lord Liverpool, "displayed a ferocity which would have disgraced the most barbarous nations" when they occupied York (modern-day Toronto) and burned its public buildings. In another instance, the entire village of Niagara-on-the-Lake had been torched and its inhabitants driven out into the snow and frost of a Canadian winter. It was time for retaliation. The sergeant received orders that the Capitol, Treasury, War Office, and various military facilities should be set aflame. To him and his men fell a distinct honour: the privilege of burning the White House, home of the hated President Madison and symbol of the American government.

That night the city was lit with red. Above the cheering of the British troops, the sergeant could hear the crackle and roar of flames as the White House was consumed, occasionally punctuated by the crack of rafters collapsing or the crash of interior walls giving way. He watched as the fire flickered, sending crazy shadows across the city. *If there is indeed a hell this must be what it looks like*, the old soldier thought.

Morning took forever in arriving, but at last a weak sun rose and shone through the cloud of smoke that cloaked the city. The sergeant, through eyes ringed red with exhaustion, watched as citizens peered out windows to take stock of the damage. Before, the White House and the other targeted government buildings had been stately icons of a confident young nation. Now they were ruins: charred beams and rubble surrounded by mounds of ash and coils of black smoke. The symbolism didn't escape the American people or the sergeant. A broad smile still stretched across his face as the British army marched away from the still-smoking city.

But at least one soldier never left Washington. While British control of the city was brief, this soldier—the grizzled red-coated sergeant—remained behind in eternal occupation of the enemy capital. His ghost is among the oldest associated with the White House and has been sighted numerous times since the early 19th century. He is seen outside the rebuilt and restored building, standing at parade-ground attention, brandishing a lighted torch that flickers eerily in the darkness. There's no mistaking his uniform or his intent.

But why does this spirit haunt the White House when the remainder of his army long ago sailed away? Was he damned for participating in the dark act of vengeance that was burning the White House? In the hellish glow of the flickering flames, did he lose his soul to some infernal entity? If so, it's likely he's a malicious apparition, full of bitterness toward his former enemies and bent on further destruction. This seems to be the most popular theory, and most people who have seen the ghost agree that he is indeed an unpleasant fellow, bent on revenge and destruction.

But it's also possible he is a simple soldier who returns to the site of his greatest pride, the one action that best defined a lifetime in the service of his country. After all, in America the burning of the White House was a villainous act, but for the British it was a matter of justified vengeance and the capture of Washington a source of great pride. Other people have speculated that the soldier may have died during the fire—perhaps crushed by a falling beam or horribly burned by flames—and that he is tied to this, the site of his tragic death. There's no historical evidence to support this theory, and thus far no documentation has emerged indicating any British soldiers died during the brief occupation of Washington.

An undead British soldier haunts the White House, possibly hoping to finish the job he started 200 years ago.

Regardless of why he haunts the property, the legend of the undead Redcoat has been passed down for two centuries now, and it seems everyone at the White House knows someone who knows someone who has encountered the spirit first-hand. Most people agree he's carrying a flaming torch, but some insist it is actually a lantern. Traditionally the ghost is most often seen wandering the grounds outside the mansion, near the North Portico, and he may be responsible for a string of unexplained phenomena that occurs there. On occasion, even tough-as-nails Secret Service agents and White House staff trained to be unfazed by nearly anything have found themselves ashen-faced after experiencing something the rational mind can't explain.

Gary L. Walters went on record with one such strange encounter. Walters worked at the White House from 1970 to 2007, first as a no-nonsense Secret Service agent and later as chief usher. In his role as chief usher it was his job, and that of his staff, to make sure every part of the President and First Family's lives were comfortable, that the White House tours and museum ran smoothly, and that the many official ceremonies that took place under the White House's roof went off without hiccup. It was a big responsibility, one he took extremely seriously. There was no room in his day to think much about the spirits inhabiting the historic building. That's why his experience with the otherworldly came as a shock and remains vivid in his memory to this day.

"It must have been in the late seventies or early eighties. I was standing near the stairway by the East Room in the hallway leading to the North Portico. I was there with two police officers. We were standing there talking, and each of us felt a cold rush of air go past us, and the doors that would stand open 24 hours a day closed behind this rush of air. I thought someone had opened a door somewhere else and created a vacuum that closed these doors, but we went and looked and nobody had opened any doors. It was very odd because, like I said, these doors stand open all the time. I just have no explanation for it. I didn't see anything, but there was a cold rush of air that passed by us." Was this perhaps the ghostly soldier making his presence known? The location certainly makes it a possibility.

But while the Redcoat most often haunts the vicinity of the North Portico, on at least a few occasions he has been reported near the second floor balcony (also known as the Truman Balcony). There is a spot on the wall near the balcony—reportedly directly above where the soldier is seen—that has been left unpainted since 1814. The blackened burn marks are intended as a reminder of the burning of the White House, a tragic but historic event. It makes sense that the ghost would be drawn there, the one place where the damage he inflicted remains apparent to this day.

Sometimes the spectral Redcoat isn't seen at all, just an eerie orange glow of a phantom fire hovering in the air accompanied by a sound like hissing snakes as the torch burns. Coils of smoke that crawl across the lawn before disappearing suddenly, the crackling and hissing of an invisible fire, the momentary whiff of burning wood and walls of heat so intense it drives people back have all reputedly been experienced on the grounds near the

North Portico and have been attributed to the ghost and the inferno he started 200 years ago.

The ghostly British soldier is one of the oldest of White House ghosts, and also one of its more unsettling. But while the war he fought in has long been over, and Britain and America have become fast friends and close allies, it doesn't seem likely that this spirit will be laying down his torch anytime soon. He's damned to restage the burning of the White House for eternity...or perhaps complete a job left unfinished 200 years ago.

Dolley Madison

President James Madison brashly led the United States into war with Britain, believing that conquering Canada would be "just a matter of marching." He anticipated a bloodless annexation. What greeted his soldiers were three years of bloodshed and, more often than not, battlefield defeat at the hands of veteran British soldiers. As weeks turned into months and then years with no victory in sight, Madison's political fortunes began to mirror those of his armies in the field. Many states, never enthusiastic about the war to begin with, turned against it and its chief architects as the conflict dragged on. Indeed, there was a very real possibility that the New England states would secede from the Union in protest. It was a trying time for Madison, but he found strength and comfort in his indomitable wife. So too did the nation. Dolley used her wit and hospitality to charm politicians,

soothe ruffled feathers and build support for her belea-
guered husband.

Dolley Madison was the Jacqueline Kennedy of her
day, an extremely popular and even beloved individual,
admired for her style and graciousness, the first presiden-
tial spouse to become a national figure in her own right.
She was so admired that she often overshadowed her husband during their time in the White House. Even in
death, her ghost is more widely known than that of her
husband. For two centuries Dolley Madison's spirit has
resisted the call to pass over to the other side, stubbornly
clinging to buildings with which she had an unusual
bond. Perhaps we shouldn't be surprised. She was, after
all, a strong-willed woman in life. She had to be. Her life
was full of travails, tragedy and turmoil.

Dolley Payne Todd Madison was born in 1768 to
a Quaker family in New Garden, North Carolina. Her
father, John Payne, once a fairly wealthy plantation
owner, had descended into poverty as a result of a noble
decision to free his slaves. At the time, the colonial government imposed a heavy fine on the former owner for
each slave freed. Payne paid the money but drained the
family fortune doing so. He then moved his family to
Philadelphia and went into business as a starch merchant,
but he failed in that endeavour so greatly that when he
died in 1792 he left his widow and children very poor. To
pay the bills, Dolley's mother opened a boarding house.

By this time Dolley had been married to a lawyer, John
Todd, for two years and had borne two children. Then in
the fall of 1793, yellow fever struck Philadelphia, claiming
Dolley's husband and younger son. Poor and with no

means of supporting herself, Dolley moved in with her mother and helped run the boarding house. There, fortune finally began to smile on the young widow. One of the boarders was Thomas Jefferson, one of the nation's most prominent politicians, who was struck with Dolley's charms and quickly befriended her. Whether innocently or by design, Jefferson introduced her to his close friend, a middle-aged bachelor and member of the House of Representatives: James Madison. Dolley and James hit it off, and despite the age difference (he was 17 years her senior), the two were married in 1794.

In 1797, after eight years in federal government, James Madison left politics behind. He and Dolley retired to Montpelier, the family estate in Orange County, Virginia. They expected to enjoy a quiet country life away from the limelight, and probably would have if Jefferson hadn't been elected the third president of the United States in 1801 and asked Madison to serve as his Secretary of State. Madison accepted and proved extremely capable in his position.

Dolley found a new role as well, one that cast the spotlight on her for the first time. Thomas Jefferson was a widower, and as a result oftentimes asked the wife of his good friend to fulfill the ceremonial, social functions of the first lady. Politicians and heads of state were bewitched by Dolley's charm, intellect and graciousness so that even though she held no official title, her star began to glow brighter than that of her husband. Even after James Madison was elected the fourth president of the United States in 1809, it was Dolley who was the more popular figure in the White House. While the president may have been respected, at least in certain circles, she was almost universally loved and admired by her fellow Americans.

During her time as first lady, she took an active interest in beautifying both the house and its grounds. It was Dolley, for example, who ordered the now-famous rose garden to be planted, a spot she really loved. No one touched the garden without her consent, and woe to anyone who pruned a bush or moved a plant without her permission. A century later another first lady, Mrs. Woodrow Wilson, learned the extent of Dolley's affection for the rose garden...and how much she hated being crossed.

Edith Wilson got it in her head to move the rose garden and ordered a crew of workmen to dig up the ancient bushes. When they showed up, spades in hand, they were stopped before shovels even touched dirt by the ethereal form of dainty woman that suddenly materialized before them. She wore frilly old-fashioned clothing and a feather-topped turban on her head, but her attractive face was dark with anger. The ghost gave the workers a good tongue lashing and shooed them away with mist-like hands. The men were understandably frightened and left as ordered. Even as they raced away across the grounds the ghost's berating continued, making it known in no uncertain terms that they were not to return. When the workers explained to Mrs. Wilson why her orders hadn't been carried out, the first lady was amazed at their description of the turbaned woman. Dolley was famous for her feathered turbans because they added height, making her feel less self-conscious about her short stature. Convinced she knew the identity of the ghost,

Mrs. Wilson showed the men a picture of Dolley Madison and asked if she was the lady who insisted that the roses not be moved. Yes, agreed the workers. Mrs. Wilson realized that disturbing the garden would also disturb Dolley's spirit, so she respectfully gave up her landscaping plans. No one since has attempted to move the rose garden. No one dares to.

Dolley still enjoys the colours, fragrances and sounds of the garden. The tranquility seems to set her restless soul at ease. On warm summer days she's often seen kneeling by the beds, as if meticulously pulling weeds. Other times, her apparition is spotted strolling contentedly throughout the grounds, enjoying the warmth of the sun and admiring the showy blooms. She never leaves a trace in the perfectly groomed grass because her legs fade away to nothingness just above the ankles.

More rarely, Dolley is spotted within the White House itself. In years past, it was said she routinely made brief appearances at state functions, ensuring all was going well and that the level of hospitality she established was being maintained in her absence. Reports of this kind haven't surfaced in decades, so perhaps Dolley is learning to trust the professionalism of the White House staff. Nevertheless, her wispy apparition still floats along halls and through rooms to this day.

Dolley Madison also played a role in one of the most memorable episodes of the War of 1812, the burning of Washington by British soldiers in 1814. As a result of her actions during this traumatic event, she wrote herself into American legend. In the aftermath of the American defeat at the Battle of Bladensburg, President Madison, his cabinet and United States Congress all quickly fled Washington, leaving the city and its people to the mercy of the enemy. Among those left behind was the first lady, who was horrified to learn that the British army was marching uncontested on the capital. There was little time left before they arrived, but Dolley displayed remarkable calmness and clarity of mind even in the chaos of a panicked city.

In their haste to leave, the government officials had thoughtlessly abandoned a number of national treasures that were housed in the White House. The first lady recognized the importance of these items and had her slaves collect them at the expense of her own property. In a letter penned to her sister during those hectic moments, Dolley made mention of her efforts to save the White House treasures: "Our kind friend Mr. Carroll has come to hasten my departure, and in a very bad humor with me because I insist on waiting until the large picture of General Washington is secured, and it requires to be unscrewed from the wall. The process was found to be too tedious for these perilous moments; I have ordered the frame to be broken and the canvas taken out." The picture to which Dolley Madison refers was painted by Gilbert Stuart and is today one of America's iconic images. In addition, her efforts saved other valuables including silver serving sets and the original drafts of the Declaration of Independence and the Constitution. The cost to her personally was high: none of her own possessions could be recovered before she was spirited away in a carriage.

Over the past two centuries, Dolley has recreated her desperate escape by carriage several times. In the deep of the night she climbs into an ethereal buggy pulled by white, spectral horses and races away from the White House. The carriage is oblivious to modern traffic, making no attempt to avoid cars as it follows the same route it took in 1814. The result is the screeching of brakes as vehicles attempt to avoid a horse and buggy that appears seemingly out of nowhere, and startled pedestrians who watch dumbfounded as a glowing 19th-century conveyance races past as if fleeing from some terrible danger. It's even been said that the ghosts seem so real that you can hear the clomping of horses' hooves and the rattle of harnesses as it hurdles past.

Dolley Madison's spirit sure gets around. Beyond the White House, she has been reported in as many as three other locations. The Octagon House, built in 1800 by Colonel John Tayloe only a block from the White House, had a warm place in her heart. After the British burned the White House, the Tayloes generously opened their doors and allowed the president to use the Octagon House as a temporary executive residence. The Madisons remained there for the rest of 1814, and it's been said that Dolley returned there in death. Sometimes she stands beside the fireplace in the drawing room, perhaps savouring its warmth. Other times, the tiny, elegant figure glides through the rooms of the luxurious manor, a whiff of lilac perfume, her favourite, trailing behind her. She nods to the right and left as she advances, graciously welcoming guests, the epitome of hospitality, re-enacting any one of the many parties she hosted for the wives of senators and congressmen to maintain morale and ensure her husband's political support remained strong in those dark days. Interestingly, another ghost residing at the Octagon House can be traced back to the War of 1812. It's said that a servant girl threw herself from the third-floor landing after being raped by a British soldier. She was found at the bottom of the stairs, lifeless and broken.

Two properties that bookended Dolley Madison's life are also frequented by her restless spirit. For a few years during her childhood she resided at Scotchtown, a colonial mansion in Hanover County, Virginia. Legend says her apparition wanders its halls, searching for fond childhood memories. Mysterious lights seen in the building and on its grounds have also been tied to Dolley's wayward soul. Sometimes they are faint pinpricks, while other times they are larger glowing orbs.

Later in life, when her childhood at Scotchtown was a distant memory, Dolley left Montpelier, where she and her husband had lived since their term in the White House ended, and moved back to Washington, D.C. Dolley, now a widow, spent the final years of her life at Madison House (located at the corner of Madison Street and H. Street Northwest). She died at the urban manor in 1849 at the age of 81. On moonlit nights her ghost is seen rocking on the porch just as she did so many evenings in her twilight years. She looks so real that in years past men would habitually tip their hats good evening to her. They had no way of knowing that the woman with whom they exchanged pleasantries was long dead. She remains there to this day, a grandmotherly spirit with a warm smile brightening a thin, creased face.

Although she splits her time between multiple residences, Dolley Madison is rightfully best associated with the White House, where she is among the most prominent of the spectral inhabitants. She dedicated years in service to the nation, creating the position of first lady, hosting state functions and bringing a welcome feminine touch to the male-dominated seat of political power. She's since taken dedication to a new level. Dolley is still at the White House, overseeing the running of events and ensuring her beloved rose garden remains well tended. The former first lady is a beloved part of White House lore.

President James Madison

Few fates could be more tragic than having a life of sadness and bitterness end, only to find another existence of such torment stretching into eternity. Such is the doom of President James Madison, a soul too burdened with despair, guilt and madness to find peace. Can you fault Madison for being a melancholy ghost? He led a young and ill-prepared United States into war with Britain, sending thousands of men to early graves. When the fighting began to go against America and the conflict dragged on over years, that decision to go to war began to weigh heavily on him. He was troubled by the loss to his nation—in prestige, in money, and most especially in blood—that was a consequence of his ambition and arrogance. Madison was haunted by the war for the remainder of his life, and indeed into the afterlife. It haunts him to this day. The War of 1812 and the resulting stain on his reputation interrupt the one-time president's eternal rest, causing his brooding spirit to linger even 200 years later when the fighting is but a distant memory and former enemies are now the closest of allies.

Interestingly, President Madison's apparition doesn't frequent the White House. When Madison retired from public life in 1817 at the end of his second term as president, he and Dolley returned once more to their Virginia plantation, Montpelier. It's this location, rather than the White House, that the nation's fourth president haunts in his tormented afterlife. His ghost is best described as dispirited; sadness seems to weigh heavily in the air whenever the former president materializes, and his pale face is perpetually a mask of despair. He stalks the halls deep in troubled thought, arms folded at his back or agitatedly running through a shock of white hair. That his spirit should be so morose speaks to the pendulum swing in fortune that characterized Madison's life, which saw him go from being revered as one of the nation's Founding Fathers to being ridiculed as the instigator of a failed and bumbled war.

James Madison was born at Montpelier in 1751, the son of a wealthy tobacco grower and largest landholder in Orange County, Virginia. He was raised in the lap of luxury, receiving a fine education and cultivating contacts amongst society's elite. He used his privileged upbringing as the springboard for a career in politics that saw him rise to the top faster than perhaps any man in American history. Madison helped draft the Virginia State Constitution and served in the Continental Congress (1780–1783), and he is known as the Father of the Constitution for the influential role he played in drafting the United States

Constitution during the Constitutional Convention of 1787 and for authoring the United States Bill of Rights. In 1789, Madison became a leader in the House of Representatives, drafting many basic laws including the first 10 amendments to the Constitution. He also worked closely with President George Washington to organize the new federal government.

It came as little surprise to anyone when Madison was named Secretary of State in 1801 by his good friend, President Thomas Jefferson. During his time in that office much of his attention was devoted to keeping America isolated from the war raging in Europe between Britain and France, and particularly to ensuring American neutrality rights. His most notable achievement as Secretary of State was supervising the Louisiana Purchase, which doubled the nation's size. At the end of Jefferson's second term in office in 1809, Madison was elected the fourth President of the United States.

When Madison entered the White House he was a man of vision and optimism, but by the time he left he had grown disheartened. He had presided over a war that did not go well and had lost popularity through his poor leadership. Madison was burdened by the responsibility he felt for the heavy cost of the war: the loss of life, the battered economy and the national humiliation resulting from the burning of the White House and other government buildings in Washington. When his second term was over, he fled for Montpelier and left politics behind for good.

But if he thought escaping the limelight for the peace and serenity of his country estate would restore his broken spirit he was sadly mistaken. The plantation to which he retired was not very profitable, and worse, he almost bankrupted himself covering the $40,000 debt built up by his ne'er-do-well stepson, John Todd, an alcoholic gambler, womanizer and thief. Madison's financial troubles only compounded his deteriorating physical and mental condition. During this time, much of his energy and attention was devoted to shaping his historic legacy, going so far as to modify letters and documents in his collection, even forging the handwriting of other political figures to enhance his own standing. It slowly became an all-consuming obsession.

His spirit was clearly broken, which inevitably led to broken health as well. For the better part of the year 1831 Madison was bedridden, and even after he was eventually able to crawl from bed once more he never fully recovered. Physically sick and possibly mentally ill as well, Madison raged over being ignored by the political figures of the day. He was the last remaining Founding Father, and yet no one had any time for him or his opinions. It was as if he represented an "old America," that of a young nation barely beyond colonialism, which the vibrant and confident "new America" of the 1830s had left behind. The perceived slight cut deeply. Saddened and hurt, Madison's mind travelled back to the past, to a time when he was relevant. He spent the final years of his life writing political papers intended to polish his reputation and enhance his position in history. Sadly, these efforts were in vain: James Madison is a largely overlooked president, and when he is remembered it's generally for his failures in office, especially the costly war into which he led the nation.

As a result, his ghost is embittered and restless. Instead of returning to the White House, which would remind him of his failings, President Madison chose to haunt the one place where he felt most comfortable and at home: Montpelier. Madison's frustrated ghost sits in his library at the rural estate, slumped in a chair at his desk, brooding over the documents over which he spent the twilight of his life obsessing. Perhaps he reflects on the what-ifs of his political career, wondering what might have been if he had made different decisions at key moments. When not sitting at his desk, the wraith wanders the halls of the refined estate, scowling angrily, bemoaning the misfortune of his presidency and final days. Even when Madison isn't seen, the heavy footsteps of his pacing can still be heard late at night, thumping up and down hallways. When you visit Montpelier, the spirit of President Madison never seems far away...and it might just be closer than you think.

Ask anyone who has ever spent significant time here and they have little doubt that ghosts exist. If you're in the majestic building long enough, you'll eventually meet the man of the house—in one form or another. Sometimes it's a startling face-to-face meeting with the ethereal former president in a darkened room. Other times it's more subtle, characterized by the faint sound of footsteps on carpet or by items that mysteriously move locations from one day to the next.

Montpelier was one of the largest plantations in Virginia and the current house has stood since 1764. It was built by President Madison's father, James Madison Sr., on land originally settled by his grandfather,

Ambrose, in 1732. Montpelier quickly became the social centre for prominent Orange County families, which allowed the young James Madison to foster connections that would serve him well in his climb up the rungs of society. The future president inherited the Montpelier plantation upon his father's death in 1801, after which he began an ambitious series of additions and renovations that weren't completed until 1808, the year he was elected to the nation's highest office.

But Montpelier's oddest and most peculiar chapter began in 1836, when Madison died. Barely had he been laid to rest when his spirit began to make nighttime visits to the manor home. His spirit grew more active after Dolley sold the property in 1844 and, for the first time in more than a century, outsiders came to live on the ancestral Madison property. Many people believe the vigor of Madison's haunting was responsible for the rapidity with which Montpelier passed from owner to owner over the decades that followed. How else does one explain the succession of short-lived owners? Montpelier was one of the most luxurious and prestigious plantations in the state, and yet no one seemed willing or able to hold on to the property for any period of time. A Virginia merchant named Henry Moncure purchased the property from Dolley but lasted only four years. Englishman Benjamin Thornton endured six years. After 1854, a quick succession of three owners in three years followed.

Madison couldn't accept that the home was no longer his private sanctuary. Resenting the intrusion of strangers, he acted out in a determined effort to make any new owners feel unwelcome and eventually drive them off with all manner of antics. It was only after his spirit settled with the passage of years that homeowners were able to endure the now-muted ghost and remain in residence longer. Madison was eventually forced to grudgingly accept that he now had to share Montpelier with others. The living were allowed free reign during the day, but he reserved the night for himself. When the oil lamps were blown out for the evening, he emerged. Indeed, many people over the years saw him walking around the mansion, seemingly completely at home, as if he had as much right—or perhaps more—as the witnesses themselves to be in the building.

In 1981, Montpelier was passed to the National Trust for Historic Preservation and an extensive architectural investigation was made into the house's architecture to determine the feasibility of restoring it back to its Madison-era appearance. The result was positive, and restoration work finally began at Montpelier in 2004. The activity stirred up Madison's ghost; it was as if when walls were ripped down they released his spirit that had been hiding in a shadowy netherworld. Workers complained of strange noises coming from empty rooms, doors that swung shut on their own, and fleeting glimpses of a gentleman who simply disappeared within the blink of a disbelieving eye. Work was completed in 2009 and Montpelier was opened to the public. The property features not just the mansion itself, but also other historic buildings, exhibits, archaeological sites, formal gardens, walking trails through wooded lots and a visitors' centre. But of course it is Madison's home that commands our attention, a grandly magnificent building with rooms furnished to be almost exact replicas of those inhabited by James and Dolley Madison.

There are some people who believe that to visit Montpelier is to interrupt James Madison in his sanctuary. There's no doubt that walking the gardens enjoyed by Madison and his wife, or pausing in the library to contemplate the former president's place in history, brings you closer to the man. And maybe he resents that. After all, he retired to Montpelier to flee the scrutiny of a public that blamed him for a disastrous war. President Madison has spent two centuries tortured by his decision to embark upon war with Britain and by his poor handling of the conflict. One wonders how the arrival of the war's bicentennial will affect his already distressed spirit. Will he retreat to some shadowy realm to sulk in isolation, or will he grow enraged and lash out at the living? It's difficult to know for certain. To remain on the safe side, it's probably best to avoid Montpelier after the sun settles below the horizon...at least until 2014 and the end of War of 1812 bicentennial celebrations.

William Roe

An entire block along the historic Main Street of Newmarket, Ontario, is plagued by flesh-chilling cold spots, unexplained orbs caught on camera, strange hushed voices and poltergeist activity. As part of the community's thriving commercial core, thousands of people walk past this block and enter its buildings every year, most of them oblivious to the whispered stories of paranormal phenomena shared between friends. How much spectral activity is drowned out by the everyday activity of a city in motion? How many people feel something unusual, perhaps even sense an unseen presence that doesn't belong, and merely dismiss it because the heritage buildings are warm and welcoming instead of dark and foreboding?

One thing is certain: almost nobody would link this ghostly activity to the War of 1812. After all, Newmarket hadn't even been founded when the war broke out. It was part of Ontario's frontier, home to a few scattered bush farms and little more. It seems an unlikely place to find a restless War of 1812 spirit. And yet, there's a very good chance that the spirit responsible for at least some of the unearthly antics that bedevil this street is that of a man who played a heroic but little-remembered role in that conflict.

Late one summer evening, just as shadows were beginning to stretch across the landscape, two friends were strolling along Main Street. Both were middle-aged women, outwardly unremarkable. One, however, had a hidden gift: she was a psychic-medium; her body was a vessel through which spirits silenced by death could speak with the living. Sometimes the experiences would last as long as an hour and leave her almost bed-ridden with exhaustion for the better part of the day afterward, but generally the spirits occupied her body for no more than a few brief minutes.

The friends had just attended an outdoor play at a local park, and since the weather was so fine they decided to extend the night by walking along Newmarket's historic Main Street. Many of the buildings there date back to the mid-19th century and feature attractive architecture so different from the plain, box-like shapes of modern commercial businesses. The women were walking along, enjoying a light conversation when suddenly the medium went silent mid-sentence, her words dying in her throat. A moment later, she began showing the characteristic signs of onsetting trance.

Her friend drew her by the arm out of the pedestrian traffic flow and up close to the buildings. At first, only inarticulate sounds came from the medium's lips. "You can speak," her friend said to encourage her. "I am a friend."

"Happy to speak with you," she mumbled faintly. Her voice was deep and husky.

"Do you live here?"

"My house," came the reply.

"What year is this?"

The question seemed to confuse the entity because it hesitated and then began muttering incoherently. Her friend continued to question her, gently pressing for details. "What is your name?" The question had to be asked several times before she could catch the answer clearly.

The medium said only one word: "Roe." And then, a split second later, her eyes fluttered slightly and she fell against the brick wall as the entity departed.

At the time neither woman knew the significance of the name, but later they realized that Roe could only mean one person: William Roe. They had spoken to one of the earliest individuals to settle in Newmarket and one of its most prominent figures in his day. Viewed as something of a founding father in Newmarket, William Roe is immortalized by the local boulevard named in his honour.

William Roe could proudly claim prominent ancestors from whom he inherited his staunchly pro-British views. His grandfather, John Loughton, was an officer in the Royal Navy who played a vital role in General Wolfe's capture of Quebec City in 1757. Loughton supervised the task of hoisting a cannon up the steep cliffs leading to the Plains of Abraham. This cannon, which Loughton personally commanded, provided General Wolfe with the only artillery piece employed in the subsequent battle and was pivotal in winning Canada for Britain. This one cannon helped shape the course of history.

Roe's father was not a military man, but rather a successful barrister-at-law in London, England. He settled in Detroit while that town was still under British rule. He was that community's last mayor while it flew the British flag, and it fell to him to hand over the key to the fort when Detroit was ceded to the Americans in 1796. The Roe family lived across the river in Windsor for several years—it was there that William was born in 1797—and then moved to York (Toronto) in 1807.

While his father carried on a successful career in law (he was one of Upper Canada's first lawyers), William, a young man barely into his teens, was employed as a clerk by the Receiver-General for Upper Canada, Prideaux Selby. William was serving in this job when war broke out with the United States, and he wanted nothing more than to join the militia and fight the hated Americans. Unfortunately, Selby would not allow it. As clerk, Roe was deemed essential to the governance of Upper Canada and more particularly in collecting and distributing tax money that paid for the war effort. It seemed that Roe's burning desire for front-line action was thoroughly doused by Selby. Little could he imagine what adventure was in store for him.

On April 27, 1813, a large number of American ships appeared on the horizon. The Americans, under Major General Henry Dearborn and Commodore Isaac Chauncey, were intent on attacking York, a town that despite being the colonial capital was a weak point in Upper Canada's defences, with few fortifications and only a small number of regular troops to supplement the local militia. The Americans landed, and although the outnum-bered defenders put up a desperate fight, by noon the invaders had managed to secure the town.

When he saw the British soldiers in headlong retreat from York, Receiver-General Selby knew something had to be done to save the colony's treasury from being cap-tured. For this vital mission he turned to his young clerk. Here was Roe's chance to get out from behind his desk and see some action. Three bags of gold and a pay chest containing a large sum of army-bills were loaded into the back of a wagon and then covered with a thick blanket of vegetables. Then Roe, disguised as an old woman in a long faded dress and face-shading bonnet, climbed onto the seat and whipped the team of horses into action.

The teenager was suddenly very frightened. He had craved adventure and excitement, to do his part to defeat the Americans, but now he wanted nothing so much as to turn the wagon around and go back the way he had come. If captured he would be treated as a spy and either shot on sight or hanged by his neck from a tree limb. His youth, he knew, wouldn't save him.

But he couldn't go back. Selby was counting on him. He had to keep going, so he drove the horses onward and away from the rapidly approaching American forces. Several times he saw enemy patrols intent on rounding up Canadian militia, and each time he was certain he would be stopped and searched. But the Americans saw only an aged woman driving a cart full of garden produce and paid him no mind.

Roe finally reached the property of Chief Justice Robinson, which was located on Kingston Road east of the Don River. There, the treasury was hurriedly buried in the woods for safekeeping. Thanks to Roe's courage, the money remained out of American clutches and was later uncovered to continue financing Canada's defence. Had it been taken, soldiers would have been left unpaid and the purchase of food and supplies necessary to keep them in the field would have been impossible. Who can say how the war would have unfolded then?

In 1814, after the war had ended, William Roe moved
to Newmarket. At the time, he noted in his journal that
the community consisted of only "two frame and several
log buildings," but it was there that the young man would
find his fortune. He and a partner, Andrew Borland,
decided that good money could be made by establishing
a fur-trading post on the Holland River, one that would
intercept Native trappers heading for York. They spread
their wares out under a huge elm on a knoll overlooking
the river and invited travellers to trade. This, according
to local legend, was the "new market" from which
Newmarket took its name. In peak years, upward of 400
Natives would congregate at Newmarket, trading furs
worth $40,000 to $50,000 annually.

The two men did well, but soon Borland set off for
richer fur-trapping country farther north to build more
trading posts. Roe stayed and prospered. The fur fort
evolved into a general store and a substantial manor
home, the Willows, located on the northeast corner of
Main and Water streets. As belated reward for his service
during the War of 1812, Roe was made Newmarket's first
postmaster, a position he would fill for four decades. Roe
was wealthy, respected, and he had authority; he was one
of the community's most important citizens. In 1878,
a local newspaper noted that "he retains his mental facul-
ties in a marked degree, and his physical health seems
very good." A year later, William Roe passed away.

Nothing remains of the orginal trading post or the store
upon which Roe built his fortune except a plaque that
points out that they stood upon the land currently occupied by 253–261 Main Street. It was along this historic

block that the medium channelled Roe—despite not knowing anything of Newmarket's history and in the gathering darkness having missed the plaque. It seems something of Roe's businesses does remain.

After researching the history of the block, the medium and her friend returned once more. This time they were prepared with more detailed questions and a tape recorder to capture the responses. Unfortunately, though Roe did make contact, he seemed far less interested in communicating this time. The medium slipped into a trance at almost the same spot as she had before. She mumbled a few indistinguishable words before suddenly saying, "Go on my way."

"Where are you going?"

The only response was a mumbled, "On my way."

The medium's friend gently nudged the reluctant entity. "Are you William Roe? Do you live here?"

"Yes. On my way."

"Mr. Roe, where are you going? Are you leaving this place?" She had to ask several times.

Finally a reluctant reply came through: "God be with you." It was the final thing the entity said before vacating the medium's body and leaving her feeling empty.

The conversation was puzzling. Was Roe reluctant to speak that night and therefore asking the medium to break her connection and allow him to go on his way? Was he in essence saying goodbye, announcing he was finally letting go of his worldly ties and moving on to another plane of existence? Or perhaps he was reliving a memory from his youth, that day when he fled with the colonial treasury. When he said "Go on my way," was he asking American sentries to let him pass or announcing to the medium and her friend that he couldn't linger long because he had an important mission to perform? Unfortunately, the connection was too brief to satisfactorily answer these questions.

But one more surprise awaited the women. When they played the tape of the conversation back, a strange static could be heard immediately after Roe said "God be with you." Then there was a gruesome laugh, starting deep down in the throat and slowly rising to a hysterical cackle. The laughter continued for a full three seconds before abruptly dying. This horrifying presence, both women agreed, was not William Roe. So it seems there may well be another presence or two along Newmarket's Main Street.

When the women asked around, shopkeepers were hesitant to share stories of the supernatural. However, these buildings are alive with energy that includes the entire spectrum of paranormal activity: sudden and unexplained drops in temperature, mysterious lights and whispers from unseen mouths.

William Roe's spirit may not be confined just to Main Street. His physical remains are buried in the pioneer cemetery on Eagle Street, and there have been reports of mysterious lights and glowing orbs around his grave. As if to support these tales, a captivating YouTube video has surfaced that does appear to capture an unusual ghost-light phenomenon in the area of Roe's headstone. This may be a coincidence, or a manifestation of another defiant soul who refuses to pass on. But maybe it's not. This video may offer further evidence that the former fur trader, storekeeper and boy-hero of the War of 1812 has risen from the earth like morning fog to chill the living with his undead presence.

Nowhere else in Newmarket can you find as much history as on Main Street. This was, after all, where William Roe's "new market" gave birth to the community that evolved into the city of today. It's only natural that a spirit or two should cling to the ancient bricks like mortar. If you listen carefully, the ghost of the town's founder may just enliven your leisurely stroll or day of shopping.

The *Dash*: Maine's Phantom Privateer

It was the summer of 1942, the height of World War II. The countries of the world were tearing each other apart, but Homer Grimm had other things on his mind. Homer thought only of the beautiful Mrs. Googie Bragdon and the next time they would share a passionate day together. Homer lived on Staple's Point and would often gaze across the waters of Maine's Casco Bay to the little home his lover shared with her husband. He longed for the days when fog blanketed the coast. On those days, Homer eagerly jumped into his rowboat and made his way across the bay to rendezvous with Mrs. Bragdon. Happily in each other's arms, they would row over to Punkin Nubb, a rocky island at the mouth of Freeport Harbor. This was their spot. Hidden by fog, secluded on an isolated point, they could enjoy each other with little fear of being discovered. So when fog began to roll in that August afternoon, a broad smile spread across Homer's face.

Homer Grimm and his mistress had only just settled on Punkin Nubb and had shared no more than a kiss or two when an ear-splitting siren suddenly sounded in Casco Bay, echoing eerily through a fog as thick as cotton. Homer and Mrs. Bragdon were startled by the wailing. They knew that the American, Canadian and British navies were jointly patrolling the Atlantic coast against German U-boats that were preying on merchant shipping and landing agents on North American shores, and that the siren was a warning that an unidentified vessel had appeared on radar screens in the protected waters. Ships and aircraft would be scrambled to intercept what might be a German warship or a surfacing submarine. As Homer and Mrs. Bragdon pondered the significance of the alert, they had no way of knowing they would have front row seats one to the most unusual naval battles of World War II.

As soon as the unidentified blip appeared on radar screens, a number of British and American warships went to battle-stations and began to converge on the contact. HMS *Moidore* was the first Allied vessel to arrive on scene, its veteran crew at their guns. It sped into Casco Bay and began firing at the mysterious blip that still appeared on its radar screen. Most of the shells exploded harmlessly in the water but one landed very near the illicit lovers, causing them to scramble for cover behind rocks as they were showered with debris.

Homer listened as the warship continued to shoot. *Bam-Bam-Bam!* The guns fired shell after shell. "What are they firing at?" Homer asked himself. Was a German sub hiding in the bay? If so, he didn't want to miss the action. Fear was replaced by curiosity, and Homer peered out from behind the rock ledge toward the water. It took a few moments for his eyes to register what he was seeing, but what he saw shocked him like nothing else he had ever experienced.

Sweeping past Punkin Nubb was an old-fashioned schooner, sailors on deck, ancient cannons peering out from gun-ports, her sails full of wind as she tore through the waves. Shells from HMS *Moidore* struck the ship, but it sailed on undamaged and the crew seemingly unconcerned by the attacking British warship. Homer saw the name upon the ship's bow and knew there was no weapon the Royal Navy possessed that could harm this schooner. He also realized that the legends he had grown up hearing, stories he thought were simply tall-tales told by old men eager to impress youngsters, were not merely works of fantasy after all. The ship sailing past was the *Dash*, Maine's most infamous ghost ship, lost nearly 130 years earlier during a war when Britain and America were bitter enemies.

The early years of the 19th century were difficult for New England shipbuilders and merchants. First, Britain and France, at war with one another for more than a decade, placed restrictions on American ships entering European ports. In retaliation, President Thomas Jefferson established an embargo of his own in 1807 that further hindered cross-Atlantic trade. Adding to this crisis for America's shipping industry were losses to marauding British and French warships, and the Royal Navy's habit of forcing American seamen into its service. Merchants and shipbuilders saw their profits plummet, and some went bankrupt. All of them blamed Britain for their pain.

When the United States declared war against Great Britain in 1812, it offered New England mariners an opportunity to vent their frustration upon the British. Throughout the conflict, the U.S. government licensed private armed vessels to serve as privateers—essentially sanctioned pirates—to raid British ships. Each ship received a "Letter of Marque and Reprisal" signed by the president and was thereby authorized "to subdue, seize and take enemy vessels as prizes and to keep or sell the apparel, guns and appurtenances." These government-sponsored pirates took the war beyond North American shores out into the Atlantic, in some cases even capturing merchant vessels in the waters surrounding the British Isles. The vulnerability of British ships naturally concerned merchants in London and humiliated the Royal Navy.

One of the most successful privateers was the schooner *Dash*, built at Porter's Landing in Freeport, Maine, in 1813 by master shipbuilder James Brewer for brothers Seward, Samuel and William Porter. The *Dash*, a fast sailing vessel, was originally designed as a blockade runner to evade the warships of the Royal Navy that were bottling up American ships in harbours all along the East Coast. In this role she proved to be remarkably successful, using her speed to easily break the blockade and make several quick runs to the West Indies, where she exchanged lumber and local crops for profitable cargo such as coffee and sugar cane. During 1813 and 1814 she made a total of three lucrative voyages to the Caribbean, each time using her unmatched speed to evade British warships and return unharmed.

On September 13, 1814, the *Dash* was commissioned as a privateer by President Madison. Now she would use her speed to hunt down British merchantmen or even small warships. Her armament included two 18-pound guns and a 32-pound pivot gun, though she also had 10 wooden "Quaker guns" intended to fool opponents into believing she was more heavily armed than she actually was. Her crew numbered 60, a large percentage of whom came from Freeport.

Although the *Dash*'s first voyage was uneventful, the same could not be said of her second. She recaptured an

American sloop that had been taken by the British and pressed into service. She also captured a small British merchant vessel, whose profitable cargo of rum was transferred to the *Dash* and brought a tidy reward for the officers and crew. Near Portland on the return voyage the *Dash* had to fight an enemy schooner, but got the better of the tussle and chased the British ship off.

The *Dash*, now under the command of John Porter, a brother of the ship's owners, continued to take other prizes on subsequent voyages during the fall of 1814. She was known as a lucky ship. Over the course of seven voyages she never let a ship she was chasing escape, and she was never injured by a hostile shot. A total of 15 prize vessels were taken without a single injury among her crew. But her luck was about to run out.

After a short layover in Portland, in January of 1815 Captain Porter took *Dash* back to sea. There were rumours of a peace treaty, and he wanted to fill his pockets with more prize money before the war ended and the opportunity for easy profits disappeared. With her was the new privateer *Champlain*, a schooner from Portsmouth. They were two days out to sea when both captains noted with no small apprehension the dark clouds beginning to gather, the vanguard of a heavy winter gale rolling in. Soon the glass-like sea transformed into a turmoil of whitecaps. Fierce winds rattled the sails and blinding sleet began to fall from an angry sky. The skipper of the *Champlain* wisely changed her course to avoid the worst of the gale, but Captain Porter still steered *Dash* on her original course. Perhaps he thought she could ride out the storm. She was last seen sailing directly into the heart of the storm.

We can imagine what tragic fate befell the once-lucky ship: the heavy sleet reduced visibility to a few feet and caked the eyelashes of the skipper and crew; all sense of direction was lost. Sailing blind, it would have been easy for Captain Porter to underestimate his speed and run his vessel aground on the treacherous shoals of Georges Bank, where the battering wind and surf would have broken her apart. Sixty men, including brothers John, Jeremiah and Ebenezer Porter, and 13 others from Freeport, were among the lost.

A few months after the *Dash* disappeared, a fisherman named Simon Bibber was throwing out his nets just off Punkin Nubb when he found himself imprisoned in a dense fog that had rolled in without notice. Visibility was reduced to just a few feet; anything beyond that was obscured by a grey veil. The sea was unnaturally calm. Suddenly, a large, dark shape loomed ahead. The fog seemed to part before the object, and Bibber watched as a schooner slid into view not more than 30 feet in front of his little boat. It was close enough that Bibber could make out the shapes of men toiling on deck and hear the creak of her lines and orders being issued by officers. The ship's sails were billowing even though there was absolutely no wind, the sea completely becalmed. But what truly stunned Bibber was seeing the name *Dash* clearly written upon her stern as she sailed by toward Freeport. There was no mistaking her. The ship everyone thought lost had finally come home to port.

Bibber was so excited he quickly raised anchor and headed back to Freeport. As he approached the wharf, he was confused to see no sailing ship docked alongside or riding at anchor in the harbour. He jumped from his boat and questioned some of the men loitering around the dock whether they had seen the *Dash* return to port. He was shocked when the men not only said they hadn't seen the ship, but also treated Bibber's claim with ridicule. Some of them thought he had been drinking too heavily, others that his eyes had played tricks on him, and a few even thought he was telling a tasteless joke. The *Dash* was lost at sea, they assured Bibber, and would never be returning home.

For a very long time poor Simon Bibber thought he was losing his mind. But then one day another fisherman, a fellow named Roscoe Moulton, took him aside and said he too had seen the phantom vessel. Like Bibber, he claimed it had emerged out of the fog like a silent spectre, and Moulton swore he saw crewmen leaning over the rails anxiously looking toward the homes they hadn't seen in months.

Since then, the phantom vessel has been seen many times upon the Atlantic, most often gliding by through a fog on her way home. The entire 17-man crew of the schooner *Betty Macomber* swore on their graves that they happened upon the doomed ship while heading into port with a load of cod. The words *Dash-Freeport* were clearly written upon the bow, and though not a living soul moved about on deck, the ship looked as seaworthy as the day she sailed out of port for her final voyage.

The most frequent sightings have come from Casco Bay, and they seemed to grow more common as the years passed. At first, they were taken to be nothing more than random sightings, but as they continued it began to dawn on people that there was something more to them. There were eerie similarities to each occurrence that couldn't be discounted as coincidence. The *Dash* appeared only when it was foggy. She sailed rapidly, even though there was no breeze to fill her sails. Witnesses say the sailors on her bow looked anxiously toward their Freeport homes. And in each case, she appeared shortly before or just after a family member or descendant of one of the 60 lost crewmen died. People speculated that the schooner and her crew returned home to sail the newly dead on their final journey into the afterlife and began to take the appearance of the *Dash* as a bad omen.

As it turned out, Homer Grimm, Mrs. Googie Bragdon and the Allied forces of World War II were not the last to encounter Maine's most famous phantom vessel. One old fisherman, the stem of a clay pipe permanently clamped between his teeth, claimed to have had a particularly frightening encounter with the *Dash* just a few short years later. His nets had brought in an ample bounty that day, so the fisherman had lingered out at sea well into the evening. Now it was dark and he squinted in the tiny light that came from the sickle moon hazed by clouds. To the north the stars pricked at the outline of hills that marked the Maine coast, and the lights of villages beckoned like beacons in the dark night. The fisherman was heading toward these lights when the water became unusually calm. The sails of his boat hung limp from the mast. As he drifted, the fisherman noted that no sound could be heard to break the monotony of the nothingness on the sea.

A dark shape materialized and loomed near. It was another sailing vessel, much larger than his small fishing boat and much, much older. This larger ship bore down on his listless fishing boat, driven straight toward her by sails that were full in spite of the stillness of the evening. Fear welling in his stomach, the old man waved and hollered, trying desperately to get the attention of the schooner's crew. They didn't hear him, for the ship continued to cut through the water like an arrow aimed squarely at the smaller craft. The fisherman watched in stunned terror, rooted to the spot, unable to move even though his mind screamed at him to dive overboard. Then cold, unending darkness.

With painful slowness, consciousness dragged him back. His eyeballs were like coals of fire in their sockets and his head felt leaden. He rolled over on his side and looked dully over his boat and out across the water. The schooner was receding from view, fading into the night. The vague memory of the nightmare through which he had lived returned to him. The vision throbbed through his brain. He remembered seeing crewmen suddenly appear along the railing of the larger ship, yelling a futile warning just before the collision. He remembered smelling the distinct stench of rot, a nauseating odor not unlike that of fish that have been left out in the sun for days on end. And the last thing he remembered was screaming just before the ship's bow collided with his tiny boat. And yet, somehow, he and his fishing boat had survived.

When describing the episode later, the fisherman left no doubt about what he saw: "It was the accursed ship, I tell you. The *Dash* riz from the waves again, lookin' just as the day she sank. On'y, the crew who hollered warnin' were white as sheets, kilt more 'n a hundred years past.

I was scared, it bein' dark and seein' a ship o' death and nearly bein' kilt meself. I watched with me own eyes as it made for land, but disappeared 'fore it reached port. The *Dash* has gone back to the sea, but she'll not have it! Yessir, the sea will cough up that ship again, mark my words."

It sounds like an outlandish tale, but those who heard this old salt tell it swore that his mahogany face, deeply tanned from a lifetime on the water, betrayed no signs of lying. Indeed, the steadiness of his gaze and the glint of fear in his bead-like eyes convinced even the most skeptical listener the man was making no attempt at deception.

The old fisherman was right in his prediction, for if the stories are true the ocean has indeed coughed up the *Dash* many times since his experience. Sightings are still being reported to this day, some by fishermen but others increasingly by the recreational craft that frequent picturesque Casco Bay. It's been a 200-year-long cruise of torment and despair for the homesick sailors aboard the *Dash*. Will the ill-fated schooner ever navigate back to port and allow its undead crew to reunite with grieving loved ones? Sadly, it seems unlikely. The *Dash* seems doomed to sail the nether-realm between the worlds of the living and the dead for eternity. Those sailing upon the waters of Casco Bay should stay alert if fog suddenly rolls in and begins to curl about their boat in an eerie dance—a ghost ship crewed by phantom privateers might just overtake them. Horrible hauntings, a cruel curse and a mysterious shipwreck are hardly the stuff of a pleasure cruise.

A Sailor's Sins

Newfoundland is the oldest settled part of North America, and as such it is steeped in legend and lore. The rugged coasts, the isolation of scattered communities, the cold waters and the harsh winters have combined to claim any number of victims. Tragedy seems to march hand-in-hand with the settlement of this wind-swept and storm-battered island. It should be no surprise, therefore, that Newfoundland is home to many lively ghost stories.

Newfoundlanders love to regale audiences with a good story, often told around a roaring hearth by lips loosened by alcohol. The combination makes for high entertainment but also inevitably leads to embellishments, making it difficult to trace stories to their historic truths. How much of the following tale is factual, and how much is fabrication, cannot be determined. But based on the number of reported sightings, including at least one of relatively recent vintage, it seems likely that the story of the Ghost of Twillingate bears a kernel of truth.

As legend has it, a wealthy but crusty and brutish old fisherman lived in the small port of Twillingate during the period of the War of 1812. Our old fisherman, whom we'll call Captain Salt for lack of a better name, was formerly a sailor in the Royal Navy and was deeply proud of his decades of service. Unfortunately, the years of harsh discipline he endured aboard ship made him hard and rigid, and when he left the service he found it hard to fit into society. Friends were hard to make.

Captain Salt began to drown his loneliness in alcohol. People in Twillingate said he drank so heavily that the bottle was as familiar to him as the open sea. When he indulged heavily in drink his personality, which left much to be desired at the best of times, became as cold as the ice-capped North Atlantic in winter. Eventually, his foul temper and drink-induced tantrums caught up to him. He's been paying the price ever since, eternally seeking penance for a horrible crime.

It was common in those days for Twillingate fishermen to employ as many as 20 hired hands for the season, whose job it was to catch and prepare the fish. These labourers, who generally came from England and Ireland, were paid handsomely for their efforts—a full third of the catch was to be divided equally among them.

Captain Salt was a cruel and harsh taskmaster. He ran his operation like a naval vessel, demanding discipline and absolute obedience of his orders. He worked the men extremely hard and grew wealthy from their sweat and toil. But his employees willingly endured because work was hard to come by and because hard work paid off for them in the end with a larger catch and more money. For several years this relationship worked to everyone's advantage. But then a woman entered the picture, and tensions arose.

Many Twillingate fishermen employed a female servant to run the household and cook for the hired labourers. Captain Salt decided to do the same. When the new servant girl arrived, he found himself stunned by her beauty. The young girl seemed to shine brighter than even the stars in the night sky. And she was a spirited lass, the kind who could make an old man feel youthful again by her mere presence.

In due course, Captain Salt began to look upon her as more than just a housemaid. He began to envision her as his sexual property as well, an object to fulfill his own lustful passions. But the girl was headstrong and resolute, and always firmly rejected his advances. Frustrated though he might have been, the captain may have been able to live with the rejection if he hadn't noticed the tender glances and stolen kisses between the girl and one of his hired hands.

While Salt would admit to not caring for any of his workers, this young man had earned the captain's particular enmity. He was a deserter from the Royal Navy, the honourable institution in which Salt had proudly served for the majority of his life. It didn't matter to the old mariner that the youngster had been press-ganged into service—one night, while in an England tavern, a navy recruiter had fed him an endless stream of booze until he blacked out in a stupor, awakening the next morning aboard a warship and already at sea—all Captain Salt saw was a man who had jumped ship in Newfoundland and hidden among the masses of transient fishermen to shirk his duty at a time when Britain was at war with both France and the United States of America. It was, to the former career mariner, the height of cowardice, and Salt would have denied him the job had there been another man willing to take his spot.

If he hated the young man before, when Captain Salt saw him and the servant girl embracing one another, that simmering hatred turned into a boiling rage. It suddenly became clear. The lass was spurning him because she loved another. One of his own employees, no less. Seeing in their love a personal affront to himself, Salt became poisoned by rage and jealousy. His mind snapped, and he grew obsessed with revenge. What could he do to make the girl his? How could he lay claim to her heart? The answer was as obvious as it was twisted: eliminate the object of her love; kill the hired hand.

Late one night, Captain Salt ambushed the younger man, striking him down with a single blow to the back of the head with a gaffe, a vicious hook routinely used by fishermen. He then dragged the body over the rocky beach and, straining with the exertion, hauled it into a rowboat. He paddled out into the bay and, once a safe distance offshore, tossed the corpse into the icy waters of the Atlantic. A great puddle of blood had by now pooled in the bottom of the boat, and back at shore Salt spent the remainder of the night scrubbing it clean to cover his tracks.

When anyone asked about the young worker's absence, he merely shrugged his shoulders and said the man must have run off. Some people undoubtedly bought the story; others did not. As for the servant girl, either way she looked at her beloved's sudden disappearance, she was alone and heartbroken. The love of her life was gone, never to return. That realization seemed to sap her will and drain the vibrancy from her soul. From that day onward, she no longer had the strength to resist the advances of the old man and submitted to his desires. In time, she became his wife and lived with him in misery. Her torment was finally ended when the twisted, heartless sea captain passed away years later. The tragic story should end there, but it doesn't.

Doomed to eternal torment for his heinous crime, the old sailor could not rest peacefully. At night, his dark spirit is said to stand at the edge of the cold water. His despairing cries are discernible over even the wildest of gales. Sometimes he looks forlornly out into the inky darkness of the bay, as if looking for something lost at sea. More often, the ghost is seen huddled over a rowboat, madly scrubbing at some unseen stain. Night after night, he tries to clean the blood from the bottom of a spectral boat, but no matter how hard he labours the crimson stain never disappears. The blood keeps coming back, and always will, at least until some unknown judge decides that the captain has served out the sentence for his crime.

Sightings of the ghost seemed to grow more frequent throughout the 1800s. Some, no doubt, were inspired more by generous helpings of rum than by genuine experiences. Yet there were enough reports from reasonable and sober individuals to suggest even to the most skeptical of folks that something was out there. People claimed the ghost glowed a pale blue, almost lunar light. He took no notice of anyone in his presence, but if spoken to or approached he faded into nothingness, as if stepping through a hole that had opened in the crisp night air. The one thing that stayed with witnesses was his eyes. They were cold and lifeless, yet seemed to plead for the forgiveness he knows can never be his.

One recent story suggests that, over time, the spectral sailor may have moved away from the water's edge. A woman named Rebecca, along with her new husband and their dog, lived in one of the small, weathered homes that seem to make up most of the buildings in Twillingate.

The house was probably built in the late 1800s, but doesn't have any apparent history of note. It's just another fisherman's house, indistinguishable from the rest.

Rebecca's dog was the first to notice the unwelcome house ghost. The dog would only reluctantly go outside by himself at night, and he wouldn't go upstairs without one of his owners beside him. He was an older dog at the time, so both Rebecca and her husband chalked his behaviour up to age. But there were times when he was so scared of something that he would run away like he was young again. The old dog would curl up on the bed and fall asleep with his owners, but if he awoke to find himself alone in the room, he'd come tearing down the stairs and race to their side.

"My dog was old, but he was no coward, so I began to get worried. But my husband brushed it off," remembers Rebecca. "Then I saw him, and I knew why my dog was so frightened. I felt a draft in the house one day and went to see if all the windows were closed. As I was passing by one, I caught a glimpse of a man with a white beard peering in from the outside. He was wearing a dark hat of some kind and just stood there, watching me with eyes devoid of emotion of any kind. As quickly as that, he was gone."

Rebecca never saw the spectre again, but she often gets the unnerving feeling that she's being closely watched. Has the lustful old sea-dog cast his attention upon her as he once did his maid? For Rebecca, it's not a comforting thought.

A mysterious ship occasionally appears without explanation off Twillingate as well. Fully rigged and flying a Union Jack, she sails into the bay and glides to a stop. She's a ghost ship, a vessel that still plies the world's waterways even though the physical ship has gone to its watery afterlife. What powerful impulse causes the ship to return? There are hints suggesting it may be connected to Captain Salt's saga. Voices calling out an indecipherable name are sometimes heard across the water, as if the undead souls aboard ship are in search of someone. Are they searching for the youthful deserter, a man denied a proper burial and therefore unlikely to have found his way to the afterlife? Or are they Captain Salt's former shipmates, searching for his soul to pass judgment on him for his misdeeds and transport him to a hellish prison to serve out his sentence? You'll find people who believe either scenario.

Today, the strange events that are said to have taken place in Twillingate are little more than legend rapidly fading from aging memory. We may never know how much of the story is true, and which of the accounts are based in fact instead of booze-induced fabrication. Nevertheless, one thing is clear: even though far removed from the fighting, Newfoundland and its people were not immune to the tragedies and heartbreak associated with the War of 1812.

Battle of Frenchman's Creek

Boats carrying soldiers with guns at the ready make their way across the river, rowers straining against the oars and the pull of the current. Finally sliding up against the riverbank, the soldiers hurriedly pile out and begin to form up into ranks. Their opponents similarly line up shoulder to shoulder, defending a stone bridge spanning a wide creek. Companies with bayonets fixed face each other and, at the signal, advance. Uniforms—red and blue—are resplendent. Bugles sound and musket fire crackles through the still night. The smell of gunpowder hangs in the air and men begin to fall. The skirmish at Frenchman's Creek Bridge plays out under the light of a full moon once again, reliving a brief but bitter night-time fight that took place in November 1812.

Long after the rifles, cannons and bugles fell silent, the ghosts of war remain at Frenchman's Creek. British and American troops are locked in an endless cycle of dying, so that while memories of the original skirmish are all but gone, its ghostly legend lingers to this day.

Frenchman's Creek meanders gently down from the wooded interior before emptying into the Niagara River a few miles north of Fort Erie. The stream is generally slow moving, but it is wide and deep, forming a formidable obstacle to a marching army. As a result, a bridge that has spanned the creek along what is now the Niagara Parkway since the very early 1800s took on increased importance during the War of 1812. The side that held it could prevent enemy movement north or south along the Canadian side of the Niagara River. It's little wonder then that the British and Americans would spill blood to control this important landmark.

Following the debacle at the Battle of Queenston Heights, the Americans began planning a second invasion across the Niagara River to reverse their fortunes and end 1812 on a good note. In the pre-dawn hours of November 28, as a prelude to an all-out invasion with an army of 3000 troops, the Americans made a strong two-pronged attack across the river. The first flotilla of American boats, co-commanded by Captain William King of the 14th Infantry Regiment and Lieutenant Samuel Angus of the U.S. Navy, and consisting of 220 soldiers and sailors, was tasked with crossing the Niagara River to destroy the artillery batteries at the Red House, a prominent home along the river a few miles north of Fort Erie. If successful, this attack would enable the main invasion force to land without facing artillery fire. At the same time, in the second prong of the attack, 200 men led by Lieutenant Colonel Charles Boerstler were to land farther north and destroy the bridge over Frenchman's Creek in order to hinder British reinforcements arriving to oppose the planned all-out invasion.

The British were desperately short of men, but because they had no idea where the Americans would choose to attack they were compelled to defend the entire bank of the Niagara River. Their forces were spread out in small packets at strategic locations. The bridge at Frenchman's Creek was garrisoned by only 38 men of the 49th Regiment, led by a very young Lieutenant J. Bartley. He and his men, who defended one of the most important spots on the Canadian shore of the river, would be largely outnumbered by the attackers. The situation would be similarly dire for the British at every one of their posts along the Niagara.

It was past midnight when the American boats were noiselessly slipped into the river and shivering soldiers climbed aboard. Once full, the boats then pulled into the current and began rowing for the Canadian shore. Things began to go awry from the very start. Captain King and Lieutenant Angus became separated in the darkness by the swift current of the Niagara River, and the boats under their command landed at multiple dispersed locations. Some of Lieutenant Angus' boats were detected and came under heavy fire before even reaching shore, leading to significant casualties among the tightly packed soldiers. When they finally landed, these troops tried to charge the Red House Battery that was their goal but were driven off by determined musket fire. Other boats, led by Captain King, landed undetected farther downstream and immediately attacked another nearby artillery position. Despite a strong resistance by the defenders, the Americans captured the position and then moved back upriver, attacking the Red House from the rear. After some vicious hand-to-hand fighting, this position was finally overrun. The victorious Americans set fire to the post and disabled the guns.

At the same time as this confused fighting was taking place, farther north the second American flotilla, under the command of Lieutenant Colonel Boerstler, was rowing toward shore near the bridge spanning Frenchman's

Creek. Four of his 11 boats got lost and never reached the Canadian shore, but Boerstler continued with his diminished force. Again, the Americans were detected before they landed and came under heavy fire from the small British detachment guarding the bridge. As soon as the boats reached the riverbank, soldiers piled out and, heedless of the bullets flying amongst them like angry hornets, lined up in ranks to assault the position. After a ragged volley of return fire, the Americans charged and drove the defenders off at bayonet point. Boerstler led the attack personally, shooting with his pistol a soldier who was about to drive a bayonet into his chest. Bartley's outnumbered force retired.

But the fight was not over. Shortly after taking control of the bridge, the Americans were attacked by two companies of Norfolk Militia that had advanced from Black Rock Ferry toward the sounds of battle. After an exchange of fire in which the militia suffered three men killed, 15 wounded and six captured, the Canadians hastily retreated. Boerstler now encountered another problem: many of the axes provided for the destruction of Frenchman's Creek Bridge were in the four boats that had turned back, so he was hindered in his efforts to break up the span.

With both the Red House Battery and Frenchman's Creek Bridge under American control, the way was open for a larger invasion to land. Fortunately for the British, no such invasion appeared and the American troops that had landed under the cover of darkness were left to their own devices. As a result, the small garrison at Fort Erie, commanded by Major Ormsby of the 49th Regiment, was able to move north and, after a brief skirmish, easily retake Frenchman's Creek Bridge, thus securing the line of communications with the main British force farther north.

At the same time, Captain King's detachment at the Red House now found itself stranded because the sailors had taken all the boats and rowed away to the safety of the American shore. He realized that there was no chance his mission could succeed, and therefore ordered his men to scour the riverbank for any boats that could be used to return to their side of the Niagara. Two were found. King ordered his wounded soldiers, the British prisoners, and as many other of his men as possible to fill them and cross to the American side while he and his remaining 30 men remained for more boats to pick them up.

At dawn, Major Ormsby's force at Frenchman's Creek Bridge was augmented with additional troops and began to move against King. Seeing the overwhelming number of enemy troops before them, Captain King and his party were left with no option but to surrender, and all the British guns were taken back from their American captors. Not long after, a fresh wave of American boats began approaching the Canadian shore, belatedly attempting to cross in support of the earlier landings. A few volleys from the reinforced British force and artillery pieces soon persuaded the Americans to come about and pull out of range. There was no further attempt by the Americans to cross the Niagara River; a second American invasion of Canada in 1812 had failed in humiliating fashion.

It had been a bloody fight. On the British side, 15 men were killed, another 46 wounded. By contrast, the Americans suffered 88 men killed or wounded, 17 of them falling around Frenchman's Creek. Sadly, the blood spilled that night still stains the bridge and its environs two centuries after the battle was fought.

Following the skirmish, the ghost of a lone British sentry began prowling the bridge, particularly on foggy, rainy nights late in the year that most closely resemble the conditions under which the battle was fought by shivering soldiers. The spectre's infrequent appearances are often accented by pitiful moans, choking cries and mumbling speech. In a frightening coincidence that lends credibility to these accounts, one of the British soldiers who fought here—Lieutenant George Ryerson of the 1st Lincoln Militia—was severely wounded when a musketball shattered his jaw, carrying off the lower part of his jawbone, all of his front teeth and a piece of his tongue. The gruesome wound left Ryerson crying out in incoherent agony, choking on his blood and mangled tongue as he tried to form words. Is he the ghost that is seen patrolling the bridge? Did Lieutenant Ryerson return in death to this traumatic event?

Giulia would likely think so. A summer visitor from Italy, she and her family decided that the best way to appreciate the sights along the Niagara River was not through the windows of a car speeding along, but rather from the seat of a bicycle pedalling along at a leisurely pace. The Niagara Recreational Trail hugs the Canadian shore of the river as it rushes between Lake Erie and Lake Ontario. When the sun starts coming out in Niagara, so too do the bikers, bladers and skateboarders to revel in the 53-kilometre-long trail. It's closer to the river's canyon walls than is the Niagara Parkway, providing a spectacular view of some of Canada's finest scenery. It's this scenery that Giulia and her family sought to enjoy.

The Italian tourists were told the best place to start was in Fort Erie; from there, the entire ride to their destination in Niagara-on-the-Lake was downhill. The sounds of cannons roaring and muskets firing at Old Fort Erie sent them on their way. Slowly, the sounds of recreated battle receded as the tourists pedalled north. Little did Giulia know that the echoes of battle—real battle, not make-believe fighting by hobbyists—still lay ahead.

When the stone bridge over Frenchman's Creek came into view, a lone British soldier stood by the railing, his back turned to the road and eyes gazing out toward the Niagara River. One by one, in single file, the family rode past the unmoving soldier; Giulia's parents and then her elder brother all went by him without seeing so much as a turn of the head. Now Giulia approached the soldier, a re-enactor she supposed. She was wrong.

The soldier turned as Giulia rode up, casting his lifeless gaze upon her. She gasped, a chill of fear trickling down her back. The soldier had no features save for a pair of soulless eyes. Where there should have been a nose and mouth, chin and jaw, there was only a grey void. The faceless spirit then blathered something incoherent, a single wet choke. Giulia was so startled she nearly fell off her bicycle. Her heart pounding, she raced after her family. She braved one last look back toward the bridge and saw the soldier still standing alongside the railing, looking out toward the river once again.

Another time, an American tourist enjoying his first Canadian vacation saw the ghost sentry from his car. He was driving along the Niagara Parkway late one night when a figure stepped into the beams of his headlights. The tourist was startled by the sudden appearance of the pedestrian and pressed down hard on the brakes to avoid a collision. Dressed in a soldier's red tunic with a musket over his shoulder, the pedestrian was obviously recreating a 19th-century British soldier. *What is this guy doing out here in the middle of the night?* the American thought to himself as his car pulled up just short of the mysterious figure.

The question died on his lips as he realized he could see clear through the soldier. He recoiled in terror as dark malice twisted the apparition's face. The undead soldier lifted his rifle and aimed it directly at the vehicle. Frightened, the tourist pressed on the accelerator and sped ahead, driving right through the ghostly soldier standing in front of the vehicle. In the rearview mirror there was no apparition, nor a body lying prone on the asphalt, only a coil of fog where the soldier had been moments before.

The unusual night was not yet over. The tourist experienced a number of unexplainable mechanical problems in what was a brand new, trouble free car. First, the car's engine simply stopped and the car slowly glided to a stop. For several minutes the engine refused to turn over. The darkness seemed to close in on the already on-edge man. He began to imagine that the spectral soldier would at any moment emerge from the pitch black to try shooting him a second time. Desperately he turned the key again and the car jumped back to life. But a short distance later, the car once again mysteriously lost all power and came to a halt. Again, it took several minutes before the car would start up again. Not long after, the car's radio began rapidly flipping channels by itself, then died altogether. By now nearly drowning in a rising tide of terror, the man raced for the safety of his hotel. Since the car had no further problems after that night, he concluded that the ghost must have been responsible. Was he targeted by the spirit because he was American and, in the context of the era from which ghost originated, the enemy? Was the soldier actually trying to kill him? It's a frightening but all-too-real possibility.

Peter grew up within walking distance of the concrete Frenchman's Creek Bridge and the heritage plaque that stands alongside it. He knew the location was steeped in Canadian lore, but as a boy it was just boring history. One night, boring dramatically became horrifying. "I was just playing on my computer as normal every night. It was around midnight when I started noticing the computer was freezing on me and the screen started flashing. This had never happened before. It was definitely strange. I was about to restart the computer when it suddenly shut off by itself," Peter explains. Frustrated, he decided he'd had enough gaming and online chatting for one night and would go to bed.

Suddenly, a chill tickled his spine and he found himself shivering. There was dead silence; no clock ticking, no cars driving by outside, no dad snoring in the bedroom opposite. Peter began to feel as if eyes were steadily watching him, boring holes through the back of his skull. The bitter taste of fear rose in his mouth. He was terrified to turn around. He didn't need to. In the reflection of the computer monitor the teenager saw a soldier dressed in an old-fashioned uniform standing behind him, near the door. The ghost stood motionless, staring at Peter with an unflinching gaze. Then, like mist being blown away by a strong breeze, the soldier dissolved and blew across the room. "I was really scared," Peter says, reflecting on that night. "I just can't get the image out of my head, and sometimes late at night I find myself imagining the ghost is behind me again."

Besides ghostly manifestations, all manner of bizarre phenomena have been reported on and around Frenchman's Creek Bridge. Strange unexplained lights often come out, appearing to visitors who are touring the area at night. According to popular account, they are blue spheres that flicker and bob around the concrete bridge and just above the water's surface. While the lights are known to vanish before anyone who is brave enough tries to approach them, witnesses who simply stand at a distance and watch long enough claim that the lights are eventually joined by the sound of muskets firing. The musketry starts faintly, as if coming from a great distance. Yet with each passing moment it grows louder, until the night is alive with the sounds of battle. Sometimes the firing lasts for as long as 10 minutes, on other occasions it falls silent after only a few minutes, but the moment the sounds of battle stop, the lights vanish from sight.

It's possible that the British sentry is not alone at Frenchman's Creek. Some reports suggest a platoon's worth of spectral soldiers may form an otherworldly garrison at this strategic location, defending against an American invasion that is not likely ever to happen again.

These eyewitnesses claim that the eerie orbs seen bobbing and weaving around the bridge slowly coalesce into the shape of British soldiers engaged in a fierce and deadly battle against their Yankee enemies. As the soldiers fall, the number of ghostly combatants thins until eventually all of them are gone, the sound of musketry has died on the evening breeze, and the astonished spectators are left alone with their thoughts and fears. It would seem, therefore, that the orbs are the souls of those who died in the skirmish at Frenchman's Creek on November 28, 1812—both from among the outnumbered British soldiers who stubbornly protected the bridge and from the American invaders who sought to wrest control of it.

One soldier or an entire company—the ghostly phenomenon continues to haunt the Frenchman's Creek battlefield. Whatever the nature of the haunting, it has managed to keep this little-remembered episode from the War of 1812 alive. The ghostly soldier's solitary guard duty and the spectral skirmishing around the moonlit bridge is an eerie reminder of this bloody moment in Niagara's history. The lone sentry in particular serves as a lasting, lonely reminder of the tragedy of war. He's trapped between two banks—on one side is the mortal realm belonging to the living, on the other is the afterlife where the dead reside. No one knows for certain who this soldier is, when he made his first appearance or why he lingers at Frenchman's Creek. Will the ghost ever be relieved of its duty to stand guard over the bridge? Or is he doomed to continue this vigil forever? No one really knows for sure.

Ghosts of the Thames Campaign

Chances are that if there's a haunting in the Chatham-Kent region of Ontario, Sheila Gibbs will know something about it. If she doesn't, she's sure to be interested in hearing about it. Sheila is a passionate collector of local paranormal stories, which she has compiled into two books on the subject (*Ghosts of Chatham-Kent* volumes I and II). Many stories become the basis of the popular Ghosts of Chatham guided tours. By eerie lantern light, Sheila and others equally devoted to the supernatural and area history lead groups to some of the most haunted homes and sites in Chatham-Kent. Participants hear well-documented stories of tragedy and death that have left their imprint behind in unexplained and unexpected events that haunt the memories of those who experienced them.

As a result of years collecting stories, Sheila is a wealth of paranormal knowledge, so when we began to explore the possibility of spectral survivors of the Battle of the Thames lurking on the battlefield, we turned to her for leads. We weren't disappointed.

"When most people think of the War of 1812 it is Niagara that comes to mind, which is perhaps understandable because so many of the war's battles took place in that area. Not many people realize that some important events in the War of 1812 took place in Chatham-Kent and that they left the landscape marked with spiritual energy that lasts to this day," says Sheila, also a passionate re-enactor very knowledgeable about the region's 19th-century history. "There were several skirmishes here in 1813 and 1814, and of course one large battle: the Battle of the Thames. The Battle of the Thames, in October of 1813, was a major British defeat that left much of south-western Ontario in American hands and saw the death of the Indian Chief Tecumseh."

Tecumseh was a larger-than-life individual and a leading figure in the war. He had brought the tribes of the American Northwest into an alliance with Britain in an effort to secure an independent Native homeland, and had proved an outstanding leader who helped win several important battles. Tecumseh's death shocked the tribes into pulling out of the fighting and marked an end to their resistance to American westward expansion. It was, without exaggeration, one of the most important events of the war.

"The fighting left a number of haunted locations across Chatham-Kent. There's the Thames battlefield and the skirmish that took place at Tecumseh Park in downtown Chatham, but there are other places as well, including private homes," Sheila explains. "Maybe with the bicentennial of the War of 1812 there will be more awareness of our area's rich history and its ghost stories."

In this chapter we'll explore some of the spine-tingling stories from across the region. But first, we trace the military campaign from which these stories were born and which culminated in the Battle of the Thames.

Battle of the Thames

During the last months of 1812 and for much of 1813, the U.S. Army of the Northwest Territory under William Henry Harrison sought to recover Detroit and capture Fort Amherstburg from British forces, commanded locally by Major General Henry Proctor. Because the region was sparsely populated and was incapable of producing enough food to supply Proctor's troops and the large number of Native American warriors and their families sheltered there, the British position depended on maintaining command of Lake Erie so that provisions could be shipped in. It was therefore disastrous when the United States Navy gained a complete victory in the Battle of Lake Erie on September 13, 1813, severing these vital British supply lines. Proctor knew that his position was untenable; he was vastly outnumbered with dwindling food stores. He had no choice but to fall back to the main British position in Upper Canada, at Burlington Heights on the western end of Lake Ontario.

Re-enactors line up alongside ghostly soldiers to relive the Battle of the Thames.

Tecumseh, the great Native leader, knew that a retreat would leave his people vulnerable to American retribution for the decision to side with the British and begged Proctor to remain and fight, but he failed to move the general. When Proctor began to retreat up the Thames River on September 27, Tecumseh and his people had no option but to go with him.

The retreat was pitiful to see. It was badly managed, and the soldiers had been reduced to half rations. The army had to dispose of much of their supplies as they went, often simply dumping them into the river, in order to keep ahead of the pursuing Americans. Making matters worse, frequent rains soaked the already demoralized troops. Proctor was alleged to have left the main body of his army under his second-in-command, Colonel Augustus Warburton, while he himself led the retreat with his wife and family and the other women and dependents and his personal baggage. With each mile marched the British soldiers became increasingly miserable, and Tecumseh's warriors grew even more impatient with Proctor for his unwillingness to stop and fight. General Harrison, meanwhile, pursued Proctor, and as the Americans advanced they captured a steady stream of British stragglers too tired to keep up with their fellows.

Proctor's army was disintegrating, and he promised Tecumseh they would make a stand at the forks of the Thames in Chatham. However, upon reaching this spot on October 3, the general lost his nerve and ordered his troops to continue marching. Nevertheless, the Indian leader gathered some of his warriors and, along with a small detachment of British troops, laid an ambush for the approaching Americans. Unfortunately for Tecumseh, Harrison was warned about the surprise attack by sympathetic locals. Having lost the element of surprise, the ambush was foiled; the two sides skirmished for a time on the grounds of modern-day Tecumseh Park, but the warriors were overwhelmed and the American advance continued.

Tecumseh continued to badger Proctor and succeeded in convincing him to go only as far as Moraviantown, where supplies could in theory be brought forward from Burlington Heights along the poor roads. Proctor decided to make a stand with his hungry, exhausted and demoralized army but made no attempt to fortify his position. Shortly after daybreak on October 5, the Americans came into sight. Proctor ordered his troops to abandon their half-cooked breakfast and formed his 450 troops (many of them young and inexperienced replacements for those lost in battle) and their single cannon up for battle. Tecumseh's 500 warriors took up positions in a black ash swamp on the British right, intending to flank the Americans. Tecumseh himself rode along the British line, shaking hands with each officer, before joining his warriors.

General Harrison's force vastly outnumbered their enemies. He had at least 3500 troops, including several hundred regulars from the 27th U.S. Infantry, five brigades of Kentucky militia and 1000 volunteer cavalrymen. Harrison surveyed the battlefield and ordered his cavalry to make a frontal attack against the British regulars. Despite the Indians' flanking fire, the Americans charged on frothing mounts. The exhausted, dispirited and half-starved British troops fired only one ragged volley before scattering. Proctor and about 250 of his men fled from the field. The rest surrendered.

Tecumseh and his followers, however, remained and carried on fighting. The battle was fierce and for a time the Natives seemed on the verge of an impossible victory, but then Tecumseh fell dead. The loss sapped the warriors' will to continue the fight. They quickly retreated into the swamps and woods, leaving the field to the Americans. The battle was over. British casualties were about 12 killed and 25 wounded. The Native Americans, who fought longer and harder, suffered between 16 and 33 dead. American losses were about 25 killed and 50 wounded.

After their victory, the Americans moved on and burned Fairfield (marked today by the Fairfield Museum), a peaceful settlement of Christian Indians who had no involvement in the conflict. Then, because the enlistments of Harrison's militia were about to expire, the Americans retired to Detroit.

The American victory led to the re-establishment of American control over the Northwest frontier. Apart from skirmishes between raiding parties or other detachments, the Detroit front remained comparatively quiet for the rest of the war. The death of Tecumseh was a crushing blow to the Indian alliance he had created, and it effectively dissolved following the battle. Shortly after the battle, Harrison signed an armistice at Detroit with the chiefs or representatives of several tribes. He then transferred most of his regulars eastward to the Niagara River and went himself to Washington, where he was acclaimed a hero. Harrison's popularity grew, and he was eventually elected President of the United States.

The campaign's most enduring legacy, however, is the many ghosts and locations infused with spectral energy that linger across the region to this day.

Tecumseh Park

Tecumseh Park is located in the heart of Chatham along the banks of the slow-moving Thames River. With pleasant views out onto the water and the dappled shade of mature trees, the park is popular for picnics and sporting activities on carefree summer days. The peacefulness of this setting masks a dark secret. Blood spilled 200 years ago has turned the park into a metaphysical grey zone where the border between the living and the dead is blurred. Sometimes, the spirit of someone long dead wanders into our world with fearful results.

"There was a skirmish at Tecumseh Park during the War of 1812, and a number of people died during the fighting," explains local author and paranormal enthusiast, Sheila Gibbs. "There have been many stories of strange goings-on in the park, and though actual sightings of soldiers have to my knowledge not occurred, there are almost certainly spirits active here. As if to offer proof, there has been some recent testing of the grounds by archeologists from the University of Western Ontario with ground-penetrating radar during which bodies, or rather evidence of bodies being buried there, were found. These remains would have dated back to the war and been soldiers who fell in the skirmish."

The skirmish at Tecumseh Park, more often known as the Battle of McGregor's Mills or the Battle of McGregor's Creek, was a minor affair in the grand scheme of the conflict. As British General Proctor and his troops retreated up the Thames River in early October of 1813, Chief Tecumseh and 200 of his Native warriors, along with some Canadian militia desperate to protect their homes and crops, decided to make a stand in the shadow of McGregor's Mills where the Thames River forked into two branches. It was intended to slow the fast-moving American army so that the demoralized British army, along with its train of supplies and hundreds of civilian followers, could make its escape. If the ambush was particularly successful, it might bloody the enemy's nose enough to turn them back entirely.

Unfortunately for Tecumseh, his plan was foiled when a local revealed the positions of his men concealed in dense woods along the riverbank. Although the ambush failed, the Natives and their militia allies fought a desperate battle on October 3. The fighting raged for two hours, and despite being vastly outnumbered Tecumseh's force only retreated when the Americans brought up cannons and began shelling their positions.

American losses in the skirmish were two killed and three wounded. Tecumseh's losses were about the same, though there may also have been some dead among the militia. It seems the dead were crudely buried where they fell on the field of battle. It's possible the Americans even

threw some bodies into McGregor's Creek. In their headlong retreat, the Natives and Canadian militia couldn't
have returned to give their dead a proper burial, so the
corpses remained wherever the Americans left them.
Perhaps it was the unceremonious manner in which they
were laid to rest as much as the tragedy of their battlefield
deaths that ensured the fallen would not settle comfortably into their graves.

"Sites of violent action have traditionally been
haunted, and it is no stretch of the imagination that this
meeting place for holiday celebrations, picnics and special events is also the favourite spot for spirits from the
past," Sheila says, referring to the lengthy history of
hauntings within the park.

The man for whom Tecumseh Park is named, portrayed by this re-enactor, may not
rest easily in his grave.

Many young people who frequent the park at night think they see things moving in the dark that can't be identified: a shadow that changes location, gliding silently across the ground; fleeting glimpses of something lurking just out of sight; sudden movement seen out of the corner of one's eye; strange lights without a source. Whatever the exact nature of their experience, all of these youthful eyewitnesses agree that there's something in Tecumseh Park that emerges when the sun settles below the horizon.

Only once has the shambling frame of someone long dead actually been seen in Tecumseh Park. It was October and leaves fell all around, like red and yellow rain. The late afternoon shadows were stretching out as Cassandra and her friends strolled through the park, talking about boys and gossiping about classmates as teenaged girls do. Cassandra was enjoying herself until the other girls thought it would be fun to begin referring to her by the new nickname that had spread around school: Jack. Cassandra had taken a fall off a bike and knocked out two teeth. A boy had decided she looked like a jack-o-lantern with those two missing teeth and called her Jack. The name soon spread, much to Cassandra's dismay. So when her friends began calling her by the dreaded name, she grew angry and stormed off ahead. The others tried to call her back, apologizing and swearing they'd stop being cruel, but Cassandra needed time to cool down.

Suddenly, for no obvious reason, Cassandra grew afraid. She could feel her pulse quickening and her heart drumming in her chest. The park, which she had walked though numerous times at night without being afraid, now seemed strangely sinister. Trees appeared to writhe like tortured limbs, and in every shadow lurked someone out to get her. Just as she was debating whether to put aside her pride and return to the safety and comfort of her friends, she saw it: an ethereal Indian emerged from behind some brush, his body glowing faintly against the fiery fall foliage. He shambled along, almost as though drunk.

Cassandra's wounded pride was now forgotten. In stark terror, she raced back to her friends and through gasping breaths told them what she had seen. Slowly, cautiously, they all approached the spot where Cassandra had spotted the faded Native. There was nothing to be seen; the ghost had crawled back into its earthen grave. If it wasn't for the tears streaking down her cheeks and the absolute terror in her eyes, Cassandra's friends would likely not have believed her far-fetched story.

Not all ghosts in Tecumseh Park are tied to the War of 1812. As Sheila Gibbs explains in volume II of *Ghosts of Chatham-Kent*, there's also the apparition of an innocent little girl who is often spotted by the young people who frequent the park after hours, an undead dog that barks from behind the walls of the historic armory, and the spirit of a young man who was found hanged in the park bound hand and foot, a death officially ruled as suicide but suspicious enough to lead most locals to believe foul play was involved. In light of the sheer number of restless spirits wandering about the park at night, it's little wonder that many people have experienced strange, even terrifying things there that leave them questioning their sanity.

Thames Battlefield

Two days after the skirmish at what would become Tecumseh Park, the Americans finally caught up with the fleeing British just beyond Moraviantown. The exhausted, hungry, and demoralized Redcoats had little fight left in them and were quickly shattered. Once again, it was Tecumseh's Native warriors who bore the brunt of the fighting, but they were so outnumbered that the outcome was never really in doubt. The Battle of the Thames ended in defeat for the British and their allies. Tecumseh's death during the desperate fighting sucked the life from his people, and they largely withdrew from the war afterward.

Despite the far-reaching repercussions of the Battle of the Thames, the battlefield is a modest one today. Located along Highway 2 between Thamesville and Bothwell, it consists of little more than a small park and a monument. The terrain would be almost unrecognizable to the combatants as it has changed greatly over the past two centuries. The dense wooden swamps that dominated the battlefield then have now been replaced by vast fields of farmland; the course of the Thames River has changed; and the wide-lanes of the highway bisect the land where opposing armies faced off against one another to decide control of southwestern Ontario. Perhaps the changes to the battlefield are the reason so few people report any supernatural activity there, despite a death-toll that included dozens of men and the dream of an Indian homeland.

Instead, the spirits of the dead have chosen other areas related to the battle to make their presence known. For

15 years, from 1992 to 2006, Thamesgrove Conservation Area was the site of Heritage Days re-enactments. At 20 acres in size, it was better suited for such large-scale events than was the small park at the actual battlefield. In addition, because the location is wooded and runs along the Thames River, it offered a close proximity to the landscape on which American and British soldiers, and Native warriors, fought in October of 1813.

The setting is so convincing that many re-enactors found it easy to get in touch with the spirit of the battle. For many of them it felt as if they were actually there, feeling the fear, anger, pain and anguish that would have consumed the men involved in the fighting. Maybe these really were authentic emotions, the result of a spiritual connection between the re-enactors and the dead. And maybe the battle was far closer than anyone involved in Heritage Days realized.

Psychic residue from the Battle of the Thames taints the battlefield to this day.

"Heritage Days included encampments for Native peoples, another for British soldiers, and one for the American enemy. It was pretty realistic and the re-enactors lived the daily lives of their subjects, so many got the feeling they really were back in 1813," says Sheila Gibbs. "Many times, those re-enacting the Native people felt unusual things happening at their encampment. There was an unusual, heavy aura that they all sensed and a variety of strange activity. This wasn't isolated, but rather experienced by several re-enactors over a number of years."

Sheila believes it's possible these witnesses were experiencing psychic residue left over from the campaign that saw the dream of an independent Native homeland in the northwestern United States shattered. Imagine the collective dream of thousands of people being destroyed in one fell swoop. Mightn't the agonizing despair of such a cataclysmic event stain a landscape? It certainly would explain why only the Native re-enactors experienced anything out of the ordinary during the 15-year history of Heritage Days encampments, even though the number of American and British who died during the Thames campaign was more than double that suffered by the Natives.

Farther upstream from Thamesgrove Conservation Area lies Fairfield Museum, another location with ties to the tragic Native experience during the War of 1812. It was there that the pacifist Moravian missionaries and their Delaware Indian converts established a small village in the late 18th century. Because they had refused to fight on either side during the Revolutionary War they were viewed with suspicion in America, so they hoped their isolated community along the Thames would protect them from violence and persecution.

For 21 years, the Moravians and their Delaware companions enjoyed the fruits of a successful community. Bountiful crops were cultivated in the farm fields, a church and school were built, and the village became a haven for travellers, traders and merchants. Unfortunately, any belief that the peaceful people of Fairfield could remain above the War of 1812 proved to be naive. On October 7, 1813, two days after the Battle of the Thames, the American army looted the village and burned it to the ground. The inhabitants, Native and Moravian alike, were cast out of their homes in frigidly wet fall weather with little but the clothes on their back and forced to walk all the way to Burlington Heights in search of shelter.

In 1814, the people of Fairfield returned and founded a new community on the opposite side of the river. The original Fairfield was largely forgotten for more than a century until an archaeological dig was undertaken and a museum established to house unearthed artifacts and tell the Fairfield story. The wooded grounds surrounding the museum reflect the peaceful nature of the former community. But all may not be as peaceful as it appears. An unsettled undercurrent, created by restless spirits, occasionally bubbles to the surface to remind people of the depth of tragedy that took place here in years past.

David Morris is one of those who experienced this eruption of paranormal energy. "David Morris is a Toronto actor who for many years portrayed Chief Tecumseh at the Heritage Days re-enactments. He was really into the role, channeling the spirit of Tecumseh as actors do. He camped on site, lived as an Indian while in the encampment and remained in character during the event," explains Sheila Gibbs. "He has stated that he witnessed unusual things at Heritage Days at Thamesgrove, but that he was most affected by an experience at the Fairfield Museum. He was on part of the property near the woods and away from the actual buildings when he felt a frigid cold even though it was summer. It was an uncanny, eerie feeling that he couldn't explain. David began to feel really uncomfortable and eventually couldn't stand the discomfort any longer. He didn't like that spot at all, and attributed it to ghosts of the past."

Is it a coincidence that an actor portraying Tecumseh felt such powerful energy a mere two miles from the spot where the great chief fell in battle? Probably not.

The Battle of the Thames was one of the most decisive, if overlooked, battles in the War of 1812. It's natural for a nightmare or two to be born of the bitter fighting and the tragic consequences that followed.

Random Soldiers

The lingering effects of the War of 1812 can be felt throughout the Chatham-Kent area, reaching far beyond the two locations where fighting took place. Numerous locations have been tainted by souls that have not been able to transition between life and death. In some cases the sightings serve to hearten people with the knowledge that there is an existence after we pass away. In general, however, the sudden collision between apparition and individual is startling and even frightful. Even when the spirit is harmless, the appearance of a ghost—something that science and society tells us should not, cannot exist—leaves a person rattled and questioning their sanity.

One of the oldest homes in the city of Chatham, located on Stanley Avenue not far from the Thames River, has long been said to be haunted by the wraith of a War of 1812 soldier who routinely appeared in the basement. This tradition goes back decades and is an established part of Chatham lore. It's not simply an urban legend or a tall tale told by youngsters to frighten one another. A recent owner admitted the home was haunted and went to the length of bringing in a psychic to gain a spiritual impression of the building and the ghost residing within it. According to the psychic, there was indeed a spirit bound to the basement, but the spirit was wearing a cut-away coat and vest. Some people worried that this finding meant that the long-held assertion that the ghost was a War of 1812 soldier was wrong. Not so fast! The clothing might well describe a militia officer, most of whom did not have uniforms but rather went into battle wearing civilian dress. And remember, several militia fought—and perhaps died—not far from the house at the Battle of McGregor's Mills.

Elsewhere in Chatham, a second home is haunted by a soldier-relic from the War of 1812. This spirit, however, seems bitter and resentful of the living. As the witness stressed to Sheila Gibbs during the compilation of *Ghosts of Chatham-Kent* volume I, he had experienced a variety of psychic phenomena throughout his life, but nothing could have prepared him for the series of frightening paranormal phenomena he experienced one night at the age of 21. Although he never saw an apparition, he had no doubt that he was tortured by one that unforgettable evening. The only question he has is, why?

This young man arrived home late one night after an extended trip away. He slipped quietly inside so as to not wake his sleeping family and stealthily went straight for his room. He was exhausted from many hours of travel, so he wanted nothing more than to enjoy a restful sleep. His waterbed called out to him like a siren and he gratefully crawled under its warm blankets. Almost as soon as his head hit the pillow he was asleep, but his rest was short-lived. He had no sooner fallen asleep than he was awakened when the waterbed began to violently vibrate. Something was shaking the bed, causing the water in the mattress to slosh madly. Though bone tired, adrenaline meant he was now fully awake.

A strange cloud of white mist materialized and began circling over his head. His heart pounded when he felt his feet being lifted up by cold, unseen hands. He wanted to scream but no sound came out. Something took control of his movements and he became a prisoner in his own body. He lay helplessly, limp with weakness. But paralysis did not deaden physical sensation; he felt the cold, clammy hands gripping him, the shivers of fear that coursed through his body, the sensation of his legs being pulled upward and his body being twisted onto his side in the fetal position. Every instinct told him to fight back or run away, but his limbs simply wouldn't respond to the orders his brain was giving them. He was incapacitated, held by invisible bonds.

Then the cloud hovering menacingly over him coalesced into a white orb that, though almost blindingly bright, did not illuminate the area around him. Instead, the entire atmosphere of the room took on an other-worldly feeling unlike anything the terrified young man had ever experienced before. The orb loomed over him for another 40 seconds or so before finally fading away.

Gradually, energy returned to the witness' limbs and he regained the ability to move, though his legs were still weak and unsteady as he fled the room. He was too terri-fied to return to his bedroom that night, the following night and the night after that. In fact, he refused to sleep anywhere in the house. Instead, he took to camping out in the backyard and did so all summer and into fall to avoid further encounters with the malicious spirit. It was only when frost began to paint the grass that he reluctantly returned to the house and his bedroom.

How does this frightening episode link with the War of 1812? When the young man finally built up the cour-age to share the chilling details with his older brother, he was surprised to learn that he was not alone in experienc-ing strangeness in the home. His brother also felt a pres-ence while sleeping one night, and had actually seen a British soldier from the War of 1812 standing at the foot of his bed. They concluded that their home was haunted by the spirit of a fallen soldier who finds it impossible to rest in his grave.

Another spirit from the War of 1812 lingers in defi-ance of death on a farm near the village of Harwich, not far from the Thames River. Here, in this pastoral setting, the eyewitness once had a riding stable. She loved her horses dearly and found the barnyard chores both invigorating and relaxing. It was while performing these labours that the woman had her brush with the supernatural and encountered an echo of a long-ago war.

Late one summer afternoon, about 30 years ago, saw her cleaning out buckets of feed using a musket ramrod unearthed on the property (at the time she had no idea it was a ramrod; to her, it was simply a metal rod that proved handy). At one point she glanced up and was shocked to see a man standing nearby. He was only a few feet away, patiently watching her work. She hadn't heard anyone walking across the wooden floorboards, which was odd. Odder still was his appearance. The stranger, who she estimated was in his mid-thirties, was dressed entirely in buckskins with a coonskin cap perched atop his head. He was carrying a musket in the crook of his arm. As the woman looked at him, a smile stretched across his weathered face and he reached out a hand for the ramrod. Still startled by the stranger's sudden appearance and trying to collect her wits, she didn't move as he took the ramrod from her. Moments later, he was gone.

Not yet ready to accept that she had seen a ghost, the woman raced outside and around the barn looking for him. He had well and truly disappeared. So too had the ramrod; it never resurfaced. It was only after every rational explanation had been exhausted that she was able to accept that she had encountered a soul drawn away from its final rest.

Interestingly, at the Battle of the Thames in 1813, and again when they raided the area in 1814, the Americans had in their army significant numbers of backwoodsmen from Kentucky and Ohio who would have dressed just as this spirit was dressed. Had her barnyard ghost been one of these frontiersmen? Did he visit her to collect a ramrod he had dropped 200 years prior? In either event, the buckskin-clad man never returned—at least not that she ever saw.

How many more spirits from the War of 1812 lurk across Chatham-Kent? How many of the soldiers who died in the Thames campaign have yet to muster out of service? And what of the Native warriors, who not only lost their lives but also their dream of an independent homeland for their people? In many cases, the legends and tales of undead soldiers are simply the byproduct of the grim power of a battlefield's mystique, but sometimes there is a very real and very frightening source of a battlefield's ill reputation. As we've seen in Chatham-Kent, not all of the war dead remain dead.

Marie McIntosh

It's long been said that love conquers all, but can it survive death? Can two lovers pulled apart in life reunite in the afterlife? If you believe in the legend of Marie McIntosh and Lieutenant William Muir, then you almost certainly hope the answer to these questions is a yes. The alternative, two young people stolen from each other by the tragedy of war and still desperately searching for each other as lonely spirits, is too heart-wrenching to consider.

The War of 1812 saw many couples separated for months or years on end, as tens of thousands of men enlisted to serve their country. Sometimes, however, this separation was permanent as death stole a husband or lover from the arms of a grieving woman. The heartbreak of learning your mate would not come marching home was devastating. For Marie McIntosh it was life altering. She would be haunted, quite literally, by the battlefield death of Lieutenant Muir for the remainder of her mortal life. In Marie's never-fading grief was born the most enduring ghost legend of the Detroit region.

At the time of the war, Detroit was a far cry from the sprawling city of today, but it was nonetheless the most important community in the region. Though founded more than a century before, in 1701 when Antoine de la Mothe Cadillac established Fort Detroit for the French Crown, its isolated location in the midst of vast wilderness ensured it had grown slowly. The British seized the fort in 1760 and held it until 1796, when they handed it and the village that had grown up in its shadow over to the new United States. Over the next decade, and partly as a result of being named the seat of government for the new Michigan territory in 1805, Detroit continued to develop as settlers flocked in and businesses were established. The village prospered until its rising fortunes were interrupted by the War of 1812.

The war was especially difficult for residents of Detroit because of the multi-ethnic nature of its populace. The people were a mixture of French, British and newly arrived eastern Americans, and the conflicted loyalties created hostility between many families in the region, often pitting one branch of a family against another. Those of British descent wanted to see the Union Jack fly over the community once more; the Americans were violently opposed to that outcome; and the old French families had reconciled themselves to American rule and were reluctant to give up the city to their old British adversaries.

This simmering brew of conflicting loyalties and powerful emotions occasionally boiled over during the course of the war as Detroit passed back and forth between the combatants and residents watched helplessly as their lives were turned upside down. It was in this turbulent, emotionally charged atmosphere that a number of ghost stories were born, the most enduring—and perhaps the saddest—of which is the legend of Marie McIntosh.

Marie lived across the river from Detroit in the Canadian village of Windsor. Her father, Angus McIntosh, was a Scottish merchant made wealthy by his involvement in the fur trade. Angus doted on Marie and watched with pride as she grew into a beautiful young woman sought after and admired by all the eligible men of the region. With her luxurious red hair, eyes as green as the deepest emerald and flawless fair complexion, she was always the first to be asked to any social gathering. Men competed for her attention, and though she was careful not to make it apparent, Marie secretly enjoyed the flattery they lavished upon her.

One young man in particular caught her notice: a young British lieutenant named William Muir. Although painfully shy, Muir found the courage to ask Marie if he might escort her to a dance. She agreed, and the two enjoyed a pleasant evening together. Much to the growing jealousy of other young men in the community, Lieutenant Muir began to call on Marie frequently and they spent many an evening in each other's company. The young officer was clearly smitten; it was evident in the way his cheeks reddened whenever he spoke her name or the way his eyes lit up whenever he looked at her. Marie, however, remained reserved as befitting the courting style of the era. She thought it would be improper to make any demonstration of her growing fondness for her gentle, thoughtful suitor.

Lieutenant Muir was patient in his courting and would have preferred to remain so, but events forced him to change his tactics. When war broke out with the Americans he no longer had the luxury of time. Muir was attached to a regiment that was selected to participate in an attack on Monguagon, a small American settlement across the Detroit River. He and his men, accompanied by allied Native warriors, would stealthily paddle across the river after dark and fall upon the sleeping village, then lie in ambush along the road for any Americans who passed by the next day. Lieutenant Muir was shocked to learn that he, personally, would lead the first wave thrown against the Americans. It was a dangerous mission, and Muir's commanding officers did not need to tell him that he might not come back alive.

News of the impending attack on Monguagon changed everything. The lieutenant realized he could no longer put off telling Marie how he felt about her. He hoped that he could get her pledge of love before he went off to battle. He was certain that if he could hear her say she loved him and would promise herself to him, he would get safely through the ordeal. Perhaps now, with him about to march out with the army on a campaign from which he might not return, the always coy Marie would finally express her affection and give herself to him.

With the spectre of imminent death hanging over him, the shy young officer found an unknown well of courage and, on the night before the scheduled attack, rode over to the McIntosh mansion to speak with his beloved. He nervously knocked on the door and smiled warmly when Marie opened it. The perfect hostess, she invited him into the parlor and offered him tea. Lieutenant Muir declined politely, coughed nervously, then dropped to one knee and blurted out his feelings: "I love you, Marie, and it would do me great honour if you would express a similar affection for me. I would make a good and faithful husband, and would devote my life to your care if only you would be my mine. What do you say, sweet Marie?"

Marie was taken aback, stunned. Even though she had suspected that Muir carried deep feelings for her, and had heard from others that he loved her very deeply, the young man had always acted shy and hesitant in his courting. Now, suddenly, he was brash and forthright. Marie turned her back on him. She needed a few moments to recover from the shock. "I do not what to say, Lieutenant. I don't honestly know if I shall be yours or not," she finally said. "It remains to be seen whether I might find another man more to my liking. After all, the life of a soldier's wife is not the best for a respectable young woman. And, as I'm certain you are aware, I have many suitors, any of whom would make a fine husband. I shall have to consider my options."

Lieutenant Muir was wounded and embarrassed by her rebuff. It wasn't the outcome he had been hoping for. Had he imagined the chemistry between them these past months? Had he been foolish in thinking he had seen playful smiles and longing glances directed his way? He was too humiliated to ask. Stunned, he stood up, stammered a curt goodnight, turned on his heel and left.

It took Marie a few moments to realize what she had just done. She had not intended to hurt the lieutenant, nor even to chase him off, because she did have deep feelings for him. It was just that she was startled by his uncharacteristic forwardness and had needed to reassert control of the situation. She raced after him but she was too late. The pounding of his horse's hooves was already receding. A dark cloud passed over her at the sight of him galloping away. How could she have been so cruel? Why didn't she simply say she loved him in return? She dropped to her knees and prayed that Lieutenant Muir would return from battle so that she would have the opportunity to make things right and tell him she would be privileged to be his wife.

For the remainder of that evening and all the next day she had a sinking feeling in her stomach. She could not eat so much as a morsel of food and found it impossible to carry on a conversation. Her heart was heavy at the thought of her lieutenant going into battle still bearing the burden of her rejection. When she went off to bed she found sleep elusive, knowing that at that very moment Muir might be fighting for his life. Exhausted by her worry, Marie eventually fell into a fitful sleep. Visions of Muir's face as he made his passionate pleas to her pervaded her dreams. Her dreams were also filled with dreadful images of him lying dead in a pool of blood. Demons of regret and worry plagued the young woman and she tossed and turned.

At some point in the night she was startled awake by the sound of footsteps moving across her bedroom. She sat up and drew aside the drapes on her canopied bed, gasping in shock at sight of Lieutenant Muir staring down at her. Marie let out a horrified whimper. This was not the strikingly handsome man she had come to love. Instead, his skin was ghastly pale, there was a vacant lifelessness in his eyes, and his rigid face was stained by the line of blood that streamed down from a terrible wound in his forehead.

"Do not fear, Marie," the spectre spoke in a cold and hollow voice that chilled her to the bone. "I fell this day in honourable battle. I beg of you only one favour. My body lies in a thicket. Rescue it from the forest and bury it in a respectable place."

Marie nodded numbly, drawing back into the pillows as the ghost stepped forward.

"Our blood was not shed in vain. England's flag will fly again over Detroit," he said. Then, Lieutenant Muir did something he had never dared to do while alive. He reached out and took her hand in his. Though she recoiled at the deathly chill of his touch, he smiled faintly before saying, "Farewell. May you be happy." Marie fainted.

The horrifying incident of the previous night was the first thing on Marie's mind when she awoke late the next morning. Had the ghost of Lieutenant Muir really visited her or had she merely been dreaming? She recalled his parting touch. Looking down, she noted with horror a deep red imprint, like a brand, embedded in her palm. She went cold with the realization that it had been no dream. Remembering Muir's dying request, Marie dressed quickly, saddled a horse and rode to the British lines. There she learned of her young officer's fate.

In the pre-dawn hours of August 9, 1812, 100 men of the 41st Regiment crossed the river to join 300 warriors led by Tecumseh. Their objective was Monguagon, where they would interdict American supply lines feeding Detroit. Scouts told the British and their allies that a force of 600 Americans was marching along the road from Detroit. They hid themselves in the woods, lying patiently in wait to ambush the unsuspecting enemy.

Around 4:00 PM the Americans came into view and the combined British and Native forces launched the attack, expecting the enemy to collapse in surprise and terror. Instead the Americans fought back, picking particularly on the British, whose bright red coats stood out among the trees and shrubs. The attackers lost 11 warriors and five soldiers, among them Lieutenant Muir, who was shot down in the early moments of the fight. The British and their allies had to break off the ambush to conduct a fighting withdrawal back to their boats, reluctantly leaving behind the bodies of their fallen comrades.

At the news confirming her worst fears, Marie broke down in tears. She went to General Isaac Brock, an old friend of her father, and related her dream and her promise. Brock was so moved by her tragic tale and her devotion to his young officer that he reluctantly allowed her to cross the river in search of Muir and gave her an escort of Native warriors to ensure her safety. Sure enough, Marie found him in a thicket, lying dead with a bullet hole through his head. She and her escorts carried his body back to the British camp. Thanks to Marie, Lieutenant William Muir was granted his dying wish, a proper Christian burial with full military honours.

But Marie never fully recovered from the incident. She never forgave herself for the way she rejected Muir, and she acquired a somber weight that she was never able to shed, even after eventually marrying and starting a family. Muir was never far from her thoughts, and on each August 9, the anniversary of his death, Marie would dress in a sack cloth and sandals and go door to door begging for money to feed the poor. It was an act of contrition for her foolishness in rejecting her first love. For the rest of her life, she always wore a black glove on the hand that Muir had gingerly touched, a constant reminder of the scar of guilt she bore.

As for Lieutenant Muir, it seemed even the dignity of a proper burial with full honours wasn't enough to still his spirit. He longed to be with Marie and was unable to find lasting peace in his grave. Perhaps if he had been able to hear Marie express her love before he marched off to battle he could have faced death more easily and been at peace with his demise. As it was, the heartache of believing his affection for Marie was unreturned grew more intense beyond the grave, making him restless and melancholy.

For decades after the war ended, the ghost of Lieutenant Muir was seen walking silently through the forest near Monguagon, still moving resolutely toward the American forces. His arm was usually raised, a sabre held firmly in his grip. He would drift through the darkness, then slowly fade from sight as his body recoiled from the impact of a bullet. The ghost always faded before his body hit the ground. While people were naturally stunned by the spectre's appearance, Lieutenant Muir didn't invoke fear in those who encountered him. Instead, witnesses felt sadness at the terrible loss he suffered in the name of king and country.

It's impossible to say whether the ghost ever found what he was looking for, but when Marie finally died of old age decades later, Lieutenant Muir was never again seen on the banks of the Detroit River. The romantic in all of us would like to believe that in the afterlife Marie was finally able to express the love she had been too proud to offer the young officer back in 1812, and that subsequently the two have found peace and bliss.

Shadow Sentinels of St. Mark's Cemetery

The lonely graveyard that looms on the outskirts of any rural town has long been a place to haunt nightmares. Even in the full light of day such sites carry with them the unmistakable air of loss and mournful memory. Weathered headstones jut from the soil at odd angles. A hushed silence hangs over the setting, so as not to disturb those resting in their earthen graves. Eerie stone statues watch with unblinking eyes, standing mute guard over the hallowed ground. Even trees seem more ominous when they grow between the stones of a graveyard, as if they might draw death and decay from the surrounding soil.

With the coming of nightfall, graveyards become even more oppressive and few people willingly push through the creaking gates into what now seems to be a sinister place of lurking horror. It's easy to imagine a feral corpse crawling from its grave, instilled with a ravenous hunger that compels it to seek out the living. In the dark of night, one's imagination might run wild enough that stories of mourners who go missing while paying their respects become almost believable. In most cases, the frightening tales are little more than the by-product of the grim power of a graveyard's mystique. But in a few, there is a very real source for the graveyard's ill reputation. In some graveyards, the dead do indeed rise as mist-like apparitions. Such is the case with St. Mark's Cemetery in Niagara-on-the-Lake.

St. Mark's Cemetery is haunted by the souls of those who died fighting in the War of 1812.

Places with a long history of violence are said to harbour ghosts aplenty. The historic town of Niagara-on-the-Lake justly deserves its title of Ghost Capital of Ontario. This town was wracked with bloodshed during the three terrible years of the War of 1812, so it should come as little surprise that spirits from the past should roam the streets on equal footing with the throngs of tourists who flock there each summer. And nowhere do they seem closer than in the cemetery behind St. Mark's Anglican Church, where tombstones corroded by time stand in the shadows of stately old trees.

As one walks through the peaceful cemetery today, it's easy to drift back in time to an earlier, more troubled era when war wracked the Niagara Peninsula. It's said that Major General Isaac Brock, commander-in-chief of the British forces in Upper Canada during the War of 1812, used to sit on a rock in the middle of this burial ground plotting battles and keeping an eye on the enemy just across the Niagara River. The fabled rock is still there, and while General Brock may no longer be, the spirits of many of his soldiers may well be. If you give your imagination free reign, you can sense the presence of these soldiers. Some visitors to the cemetery actually see or hear them.

St. Mark's Cemetery is one of the oldest cemeteries anywhere in Ontario. It was established in 1792 to serve the village and its surrounding area. Centuries before, the grounds were used as a burial site by Native Americans, dozens, perhaps hundreds of whom were laid to rest in these hallowed grounds and then disturbed when the soil was dug up to bury European settlers. The earliest recognizable headstone dates back to 1794, and over the next few decades a handful of others joined it as old age, accidents and disease claimed members of the small community. Then came a deluge of interments during the War of 1812, and suddenly somber headstones were popping up from the grass like trilliums in springtime. Many of those who died fighting under the British banner ended up in St. Mark's. Laid to rest alongside them were the innocents who froze to death when the town was razed by the Americans in December of 1813.

St. Mark's was quite literally scarred by that conflict of long ago. The church, only four years old when the war erupted, was pressed into service as a hospital to treat soldiers gruesomely wounded in battle. Among the common wounds were limbs shattered by bullets and infected with gangrene. Surgeons often had no recourse but to amputate.

The grim marks left by cleaving axes, deep gashes as much as six inches in length, can still be seen in the surfaces of flat tombstones that served as improvised operating beds. Many of these unfortunate soldiers never recovered from the primitive surgery, dying from either loss of blood or infection. They were buried in the cemetery, perhaps only a few feet from where the amputation occurred. Then, before the Americans retreated from Niagara-on-the-Lake toward the end of 1813, they sacrilegiously torched the church, forcing the shocked community to hold ceremonies for fallen soldiers in a fire-blackened shell of a building before burial. It was hardly a fitting setting to pay respects to young men who heroically gave their lives in defence of a nation.

Tragically, it seems there is no repose for some of these men who were cut down in battle in the prime of their lives. Cold blasts of air, the unsettling feeling of someone standing at your shoulder and whispered voices have all been known to alarm even skeptical visitors who find themselves standing in the cemetery as twilight creeps over the surrounding community. Many people say that spectral soldiers from this blood-soaked era walk the cemetery ground to this day. Often the ghosts are missing an arm or simply fade away at the hip, evidence perhaps that the men endured the agony of amputation before succumbing to their wounds. Other witnesses have seen ghost lights dancing around the tombstones, casting an eerie glow in an already macabre setting. Many people have been terrorized by the sounds of disembodied screams or have detected a rotting smell, like that which can only come from a corpse. There are even reports of spectral Indians lurking in the shadows, spirits who were undoubtedly riled by the white man's burials that desecrated their sacred ground.

Psychics and other people sensitive to the rhythms of the spirit world have had even more troubling experiences among the leaning headstones of St. Mark's Cemetery. Pauline Raby, a psychic who assisted paranormal researcher John Savoie in researching the book *Shadows of Niagara*, reported feeling pains in her limbs while exploring the site. She accounted for it by suggesting the discomfort was a manifestation of the suffering the ghosts themselves continue to endure 200 years after their death. And Raby was adamant that it wasn't merely one or two ghosts she sensed. In her estimation there were numerous spirits lingering in the graveyard, and most of them were War of 1812-era soldiers. Many eyewitnesses would agree with her assessment.

One recent experience is particularly chilling. It was midsummer and a woman was visiting the cemetery to pay respects to her departed father. The sun was high in the sky, and even the ancient trees that shade the cemetery did little to ward off the oppressive heat. Suddenly, the woman noted a severe and unexplainable drop in temperature. Dirt and leaves kicked up, dancing in a tight circle before her, but there was no wind—nothing to create the miniature dust devil. In the midst of the swirling debris a solemn, smoky soldier appeared. He was dressed in the uniform of a time long past, his face etched with sadness. The ghost stared directly at her with soulless eyes and moved his mouth as though to speak, but no sound came out. For a single heartbeat the woman knew the full truth of terror, but just as suddenly as the ghost had appeared he simply faded away.

The woman was left alone in the cemetery with nothing but questions about what the ghost was so urgently trying to tell her. If only she could have heard the spirit, we might have gained some understanding of who he was and why he lingers so long after his death. He and the other men-at-arms laid to rest in St. Mark's Cemetery have served their country for two centuries now, a ghostly company defending Niagara-on-the-Lake from a nonexistent foe.

At least one account suggests that the ghostly soldiers bound to the cemetery have become disillusioned and embittered with their eternal obligation to king and country. The witness, a middle-aged man, was driving past St. Mark's Church one night when he saw a strange orange glow emanating from the lifeless depths of the cemetery. It was faint but distinct. Intrigued, he pulled over to the side of the road, climbed out of the car and cautiously crept into the graveyard for a closer look. What he saw stunned him.

Standing amid the weathered gravestones was a dark-haired man in what appeared to be an old-fashioned military uniform. He stood motionless, staring down at a spot on the ground. The mysterious figure held a lighted candle in one hand, and it was the flickering flame that cast the ghostly illumination. The figure looked sad, the candle's glow accentuating his tormented features. A shiver ran down the witness' spine when he realized that the ghost lacked an arm, his appendage simply fading away near the elbow. As if he had suddenly become aware he was no longer alone, the ghost looked up and his hollow eyes met those of his trembling audience. The man was terrified by what he saw. Looking back at him was a face with white skin stretched tight over protruding bones. He sensed within the ghost a jealous longing for a life long past, and it frightened him like nothing he had ever before experienced. To the man's immense relief, in only a few moments the ghostly image began to fade from view. That wasn't the last of the unsettling encounter, however. Far from it.

"I think I brought the ghost home with me that night because weird, unexplainable things began happening in my house—things that had never happened before," the eyewitness reported. The paranormal activity began with a general sense of unease, as if someone was watching him all the time. Occasionally, there would even be momentary touches. Several nights the man awoke from sleep convinced someone was standing over the bed, looming with sinister intent. But when his eyes finally focused, he'd always find himself alone in his bedroom. And yet, the uneasy feeling persisted, preventing him from returning to sleep for the remainder of the night whenever it happened.

The ghost wouldn't simply make its presence known at night, however. On two occasions the man returned home to find a deadbolt across his front door. Because the bolt could only be locked from the inside and he lived alone, the man could find no logical explanation. He had to crawl through a window both times, and in a fit of frustration removed the deadbolt after the second incident. It seemed as if the ghost had been trying to keep the man out of his own home, though why remains a mystery.

Also a mystery is what drove the ghost away, for shortly after the deadbolt was removed the oppressive atmosphere in the home was suddenly lifted. The man hasn't experienced any unusual activity since then, for which he is thankful.

We can validate the varied stories coming out of St. Mark's Cemetery, since we too came face to face with a spectral reminder of the graveyard's bloody history. It was a dismal fall day when we came to visit the haunted cemetery. The air was chilled; a light mist clung to the ground and dark clouds weighed down on us from the moody October sky. If St. Mark's did in fact have any spirits lingering, it would be a day like this that they just might make their presence known.

We took a few moments to appreciate St. Mark's Church, itself a mystical building and a fine monument to years gone by. Standing beneath its proud spire, we could easily understand why this historic House of God has been beloved by generations of worshippers. We were anxious to go inside but the doors were regrettably locked. The splendid interior, and the spectral monk and ghostly nuns that apparently reside within, would have to wait for another day.

We made our way to the back of the church, where the cemetery stretches out toward the Niagara River. It didn't take long to locate the gravestones upon which the amputations were supposed to have been performed 200 years ago. There were two of them, both about six feet long and three feet wide and dated back to the late 1700s. Both were defaced by deep gouges, obviously made by a sharp object delivered with considerable force.

The marks, wedge-shaped and measuring four to six inches in length, were consistent with what one would expect an axe blade to make.

Maria leaned down to get a better look at the markings, gingerly running her fingers over them. She remarked that the stone felt unusually cold to the touch, like a block of ice. The sensation was soon replaced by something else, flashes of insight that were unusually detailed and left her disturbed. A scene began to play out before her eyes, like a series of sepia-tone photos flashing by. Maria saw three black-clad nuns standing nearby, holding their rosaries in wrinkled hands. She saw the face of a doctor etched with grim determination, and watched as a young soldier with shattered legs writhed in agony atop the tombstone just inches from her hands. She heard screaming and a chorus of prayers as the doctor raised an axe high above his head and then brought it down...

The marks—and the painful memories—from long-ago amputations are still evident on some of the gravestones in the cemetery.

The image faded in that moment, but Maria was left with a gnawing ache in her legs that endured for hours. She believes that she witnessed the replaying of an event that occurred over a hundred years before she was even born, and that the pain she endured for the remainder of the day was the psychic residue of an ancient amputation. When she spoke of her experience her voice was choked with emotion, but what really added believability was her vivid description of the soldier's garb. Maria, who knows nothing of military history, accurately described the uniforms of the Queen's York Rangers, right down to the short green jacket (unusual at a time when most British soldiers wore the ubiquitous red coat), white leggings and tall shako. We were both absolutely convinced that Maria was just the most recent in a long string of individuals to have unexplainable, often terrifying experiences at St. Mark's Cemetery.

Despite its troubled history, St. Mark's Cemetery bears its wounds and sorrows like badges of honour, reminders of a painful era in Canadian history. The faded headstones from the War of 1812 look sturdy enough to stand another 200 years, and it's likely that as long as they remain, so too will several ghostly soldiers who met an agonizing end in the aftermath of battle. These soldiers do not sleep peacefully in their hallowed ground, so if you find yourself in the cemetery on a moody, overcast fall day or as twilight begins to creep its shadows over landscape, keep watch for somber apparitions of undead soldiers to materialize and steel yourself for the shock to your senses.

Mournful Mother of Lewiston

It was just before the War of 1812 that a young, newly married couple settled on a farmstead near Lewiston, New York. They'd chosen the location of their farm well. The land was fertile and ideal for growing crops. Water was plentiful. And at night, they could sit on the porch of their cabin and enjoy spectacular sunsets over the Niagara River as they thought about all the dreams they shared. In their eyes this was the perfect place to settle and start the family that they longed for. The couple was just starting out in life and didn't have a lot of money, but they were very much in love and had high hopes for the future. They envisioned vast fields of golden wheat swaying gently in the wind, pens with well-fed pigs, coops full of chickens, bountiful orchards of ripe fruit and a vegetable garden crowded with all kinds of produce. Most of all, they envisioned a family of little ones playing and giggling happily.

It wasn't long after they were settled that they learned she was with child. And when a baby boy emerged nine months later they held each other close, glowing in the happiness of the moment. It was a blissful start to a lifetime of happiness together. Life was perfect for this young couple so in love.

And then the War of 1812 erupted. The husband decided that it was his patriotic duty to join the militia and fight on behalf of his country. His wife pleaded with him to reconsider, fearing that he might be terribly hurt or even killed in battle and leave their child fatherless. But he couldn't be dissuaded. Only a coward would not stand up and fight for his country, and he was no coward. When the day for his departure came, the young man awoke at dawn. He kissed his wife gently on her lips and whispered in her ear that all would be well, that it wouldn't be long before he was in her arms again. He softly walked over to the crib, leaned in and kissed his son on his head. His heart ached as he turned and walked away from the family he loved so dearly. As the cabin's door closed behind him, a wave of sadness welled up from deep within. He walked as quickly as possible from the house and never looked back, fearing that if he snuck one last glance he'd change his mine and return to those he loved.

Months later, the woman was outside one day scrubbing clothes when she turned to see a figure in the distance. Hoping it was her beloved, she waved happily. She cast an affectionate glance at her baby boy, sleeping quietly nearby on a blanket spread over the grass. She couldn't wait to see the pride in her husband's face as he picked up his son and marvelled at how much he'd grown. But suddenly her excitement turned to fear. It wasn't her husband approaching from the wood line, but two fearsomely painted Native warriors. They were thin men, with evil-looking eyes in bony faces. Both were holding knives in their hands. Seeing that they had been spotted, the warriors let out a bloodcurdling scream and raced toward her.

The young woman looked at their knives and felt a cold lump grow in the pit of her stomach. Fearful for her infant son, still sleeping peacefully on his blanket, she dropped her laundry basket and ran for him. Even with a speed born of desperation she wasn't fast enough reaching her baby. The Natives arrived first. One snatched him up with his dirty hands, while the other grabbed for her. One hand clamped down over her mouth, the other brought a knife up to her throat. She could feel the cold steel against her flesh. The stench of him was overwhelming.

She did the only thing she could and bit down hard on his palm. The man swore in pain. The taste of blood filled her mouth until he let go. The woman screamed and stumbled toward the house. She slammed the door closed behind her and barred it without even thinking about her baby until he began wailing, terror clear in his cries. The young mother was horrified, not out of fear for the Natives but because she couldn't believe she ran without her child. The baby's screams pierced her ears as tears filled her eyes. Then, just as she had built up the courage to go and try to recover her baby, the wailing stopped. Heartbroken, the woman slumped to the floor, tears now streaming down her cheeks as a sick feeling crept through her body and chilled her soul. She knew she wouldn't be holding her baby in her arms ever again.

But the grief-stricken mother's ordeal wasn't over. The murderous men pounded against the door, throwing their weight against it time after time in an attempt to break in. When they realized the door was too strongly built, they began to scale the roof. The woman's heart stuck in her throat. She knew they intended to climb down the chimney, so with trembling hands she dumped her straw bed into the hearth. The fire fed hungrily on the dry straw, sending thick smoke and roaring flames up the chimney. The men screamed in agony, dropping down into the fire-place and rolling out onto the cabin floor. Their clothes and hair were on fire, the stench filling the room. They stumbled about, mindless with pain, screaming like the devil himself. The woman looked on them without the slightest shred of pity. She picked up an axe and struck them down, cleaving their skulls with a strength born of hatred.

It was only later, as she lay with the lifeless body of her baby cradled in her arms, that she noticed something unusual about the Natives. Both men had pale eyes and a growth of stubble upon their cheeks. She knew Indians didn't have facial hair, nor did they have blue eyes. After washing the soot and war-paint from their faces, she recognized them as two pro-British neighbours who had previously accosted her on several occasions because of her husband's decision to fight for the United States. She was sickened by the war and turned her back on the men.

Still in shock, she could not bring herself to bury her child. She lay the dead child in his crib and closed his eyes. She placed a doll in his lifeless arms. Beneath his wasting form, the linens grew damp and stained yellow by bodily fluids that had slowly leaked out of him as time passed. When neighbours came calling on the young mother and her child they knocked on the door for several minutes without an answer. Just as they were about to leave, the reek of decay seeping out of the cottage alerted them that something was wrong. They pushed open the door and stepped inside to find the woman, gaunt, unwashed, unfed and ungroomed for what looked like days, gently rocking the crib and the decomposing baby at rest within. Two dead bodies lay nearby, their skulls cleaved in, blood and brain matter spilling out and staining the wooden floorboards. The gruesome sight and horrid stench nearly caused them to retch. Neither man had ever encountered anything so sickening.

The two neighbours decided the woman could not stay in this house. She was clearly in need of help. One of the men agreed to take her into his home until her husband returned from the war. But the young mother would not part from the cradle, so the man placed both her and the cradle—including the baby wasting away within—in a backroom of his cabin. She watched over the cradle, day and night, for weeks on end. Not for a moment did she leave its side. Meals were brought to her and chamber pots were placed near her. The woman scarcely slept because she didn't want to turn her back on the baby ever again. Her long hair grew dull and tangled, her skin grey and lifeless. Slowly the will to live was slipping from her. She died of a broken heart.

That was a long time ago. Today, the identities of those involved in the story have been forgotten and no one remembers the exact location of this brutal scene. But folklore says that the grieving mother and her assailants never left. Tales from the 19th century suggest she still mourned the loss of her son even after she joined him in death. A lost soul, her ghost is said to have appeared in both her home and the home of the neighbour who took her in (and indeed within the homes which were built upon the foundations of these primitive cabins later in the century). Hers is a melancholy ghost. She was said to be seen either rocking an invisible cradle or sobbing inconsolably as she wandered about the house.

Some people might consider this story to be mere folklore, a chilling tale designed to frighten children or entertain friends huddled around a fire on a stormy night. But a horrifying experience that took place about 30 years ago suggests there may be more to it than mere fantasy. Deanna, now a middle-aged mother, was so deeply scarred by her childhood encounter with a ghost that she's rarely spoken about it.

"As a girl, I lived in an older home in Lewiston. I was horribly afraid of the dark, like most children are I suppose, but I also hated the silence of my home late at night and I swore frightening things hid in every shadow. As a consequence, I would routinely crawl into bed with Mom and Dad in the middle of the night, and if I had to go to the bathroom after being tucked in I called them to take me. There was something not right about the house. Even as a girl I could sense it," Deanna recalls today.

One night, when she was about seven or eight, she had to go to the bathroom and found the courage to go without calling someone to escort her. She crawled out of bed and cautiously walked out into the hall. She was just getting her eyes adjusted to the dim light when she felt a cold breeze blow by her. Her eyes grew wide when a woman materialized out of the darkness.

"She was at the far end of the hall and looked directly at me. I've never been more frightened in my life. She was a young woman wearing an old-fashioned and well-worn plaid dress and it looked like she was wearing a bonnet on her head," Deanna says. "I tried to call for my mom and dad, but couldn't. No sound would come out no matter how hard I tried to scream. The woman started to come toward me, but she didn't float like a ghost is supposed to. Her movements were jerking and erratic. I couldn't move my legs. I was frozen in place. The woman came very close and opened her arms as if she wanted to pick me up. Just as her hands were about to touch me she suddenly disappeared. I can still remember how sad she looked, and even talking about it makes my hair stand on end."

The youngster ran back to her bed, dove under the covers and remained there for the rest of the night. Dawn was agonizingly long in coming. In the morning, Deanna tearfully told her mom that she had seen a ghost, but her mother dismissed her out of hand. "There is no such thing as ghosts, and you shouldn't make up stories," she was told in a stern voice that let her know this was the last word on the subject. Deanna never again raised the subject with her parents, but her mother's assurance that ghosts didn't exist didn't help allay her fears. For years afterward she slept with a blanket over her head and refused to go to the bathroom at night.

So it would seem that the heart-breaking ghost story that most people dismiss as folklore may indeed have a basis in fact. Deanna's experience and those which tradition says took place in the distant past are too similar to be coincidence. There's little doubt that the mother's tortured wraith did deny the call of the grave, and that she still endures today.

The mournful mother's time to leave this existence has long past. How long will she continue to grieve for her baby, murdered by men driven to hatred by the horror of war? Tragically, in her madness she has not realized that as long as she remains earthbound she will never be reunited with him. She proves that a mother's love is undying, extending beyond the grave, but ironically it's this all-consuming love that prevents her from finding solace in death.

Battle of Chippawa

Night had settled heavily on the landscape. Above, a quarter moon hazed by clouds gave off only a feeble light. Without warning, the darkness was lit up by flaming muskets as dense rows of grim-faced soldiers faced off against one another. Smoke filled the field as the three-quarter-inch musket balls whistled through the still night air. Soldiers quickly took the next cartridge from their ammunition pouch and began the labourious process of reloading, all the while ignoring the shouts of the enemy, the musket bullets flying toward them, the screaming of horses and the calm voices of officers ordering the slaughter. It was mechanical work, clockwork killing. Fire, reload, present, fire, until their faces were blackened, their eyes stinging with the grains of powder thrown up by the priming just inches from their cheeks, and their shoulders bruised by the kick of the gun. The ground was soon littered with bodies.

Steve and Pierre, lifelong friends, unexpectedly found themselves caught between the warring armies. As bullets flew overhead they reflexively dropped to the ground, pressing their bodies flat against the damp fall grass. They screamed in terror, but their voices were drowned out by the thunderous sounds of battle being waged all around them. Both teenagers were certain an errant shot would eventually hit them, but they were frozen by fear and unable to crawl out of the line of fire.

Then, through eyes wide with fright, Steve and Pierre watched as suddenly the soldiers seemed to waver, becoming insubstantial, little more than wisps of bone-white smoke, and were carried away on a chill autumn breeze. Where just moments before had stood hundreds of combatants locked in mortal combat, where dozens of dead and wounded had littered the ground where they had fallen, there was now nothing but grass and, in the distance, a memorial to the Battle of Chippawa. Steve and Pierre, who had been rooted to the spot by terror throughout the fighting, now regained control of their limbs. Springing to their feet, they ran from the scene on legs made rubbery by fear, every once in a while throwing panicked looks over their shoulders to ensure the spectral soldiers hadn't reappeared to fire their weapons in their direction, relieved when the battlefield remained empty and eerily silent. The Battle of Chippawa was over, again… some 190 years after it had originally been fought on July 5, 1814.

The dead do not lie peacefully in their graves at Niagara Falls' Chippawa battlefield, nor do they seem to realize that a treaty has long since ended the war in which they fought and died. Sometimes, late at night, long-dead soldiers claw forth from their earthen graves to march and do battle once more. Cannons roar, muskets fire, the wounded cry out in pain: a 200-year-old battle relives itself under the pale blue light of the moon, the combatants doomed never to lay down their arms. The Chippawa battlefield is a site of suffering and sacrifice, where over 100 bodies lie in unmarked graves, so is it little wonder that even after the muskets, cannons and drums have fallen silent the ghosts of war return?

The original Battle of Chippawa took place in the stifling heat of the summer of 1814 and represented the opening engagement of that year's Niagara campaign, the longest and bloodiest military operation of the War of 1812. On the morning of July 3, American Major-General Jacob Brown led an army across the Niagara River against Fort Erie. The 38-year-old Brown was an unlikely soldier. Born of Quaker origins in Bucks County, Pennsylvania, he was in peacetime a schoolteacher in upstate New York who dabbled in military matters as an officer in the militia. Though not with the regular American army, he was nonetheless a resourceful leader with a string of victories to his name, and quickly added one more at Fort Erie. The fort's 170-man garrison put up only a token resistance to the Americans before surrendering, throwing down their weapons and marching sullenly into captivity. For the Americans, it was a glorious Fourth of July.

When the British commander in Niagara, Major-General Phineas Riall, heard about the invasion, he rushed south to repel the Americans. At the same time, Brown was advancing north from Fort Erie. The two armies were on a collision course that would result in one of the bloodiest days of the war.

The morning of July 5 saw the two armies eyeing one another from opposite shores of the Chippawa River. Riall was itching for a fight. The younger son of a wealthy Anglo-Irish banking family, he had entered the army at age 18 in 1794 but had yet to see any significant action. That day Riall rashly decided to attack. With about 2000 men, he moved against an enemy he believed to be similar in size and consisting of untrained militia, when in fact the Americans numbered 3500 men, the majority of whom were disciplined regular troops.

The British crossed the Chippawa River and marched through the fields of Samuel Street's farm toward the American positions, expecting the enemy to scatter as they generally did when faced with the cold steel of bayonets wielded by red-coated British soldiers. Riall was stunned when the enemy proved to be sturdy soldiers who were as well-trained as his own men, able to withstand a musket volley and calmly return fire in kind. The Americans didn't break and scatter at the first shot of artillery, as he had arrogantly predicted they would, but rather formed lines and faced the British head-on. They took the worst the Redcoats could deliver and handed it right back, causing the British general to supposedly exclaim, "Why, these are regulars, by God!"

The combined fire of the American artillery and musketry halted the British attack. The battle became a stationary, close-range fire fight. Both lines stood and fired; reloaded and fired; reloaded and fired. It was, in the words of Lieutenant John Stevenson, a "scene of carnage." The firing soon engulfed both lines in dense clouds of smoke. The cries of the wounded and dying were drowned out by the cacophony of artillery and musketry. The officers had long stopped controlling the volleys. Now each man fired as fast as he could, ignoring the fresh blood that made the grass slippery and the screams, the terrible agony, of brothers-in-arms collapsing when a bullet struck home. It was warfare at its ghastliest. After 25 minutes of this close-range combat, and finally realizing he was heavily outnumbered, Riall acknowledged defeat and ordered a retreat which was completed in good order and without American pursuit.

The fighting, which had started early in the morning, had lasted until nearly six o'clock in the evening. By the time the last gun fell silent on the Chippawa battlefield, it was the Americans who were standing victorious, with some 300 casualties, while the British slinked from the battlefield after suffering over 100 dead, 321 wounded and 46 captured. It was the most sanguinary encounter of the war so far. The Americans buried their dead enemies on the field where they fell, in unmarked graves and with no ceremony to mark their passing. For two days, surgeons dealt with the gruesome aftermath of battle, amputating shattered limbs and prying musket balls from shredded flesh, adding more blood to a field already stained crimson.

What lay ahead for the two armies was an even bloodier fight, the Battle of Lundy's Lane, fought on July 25, 1814, which has long overshadowed the Battle of Chippawa. This decisive engagement turned back the invaders and saved Niagara. Within a matter of weeks the Americans had retreated to their side of the Niagara River and for the remainder of the war didn't seriously threaten Canada again. The Battle of Lundy's Lane, a defining moment in the war, is well-remembered by Canadian history whereas the Battle of Chippawa is largely overlooked.

Because it was cast in the shadow of a larger battle, and undoubtedly also because it was a British-Canadian defeat, little was done to commemorate the Battle of Chippawa or those who had fallen there. The battle and the dead who lay in shallow graves upon the fields where it was fought were soon forgotten. Years turned to decades, and the mortal drama that played itself out on the Chippawa battlefield was buried under the passage of time and the farmer's plow.

Until, that is, very recently, when the battlefield was reclaimed as a place of national importance. The Niagara Parks Commission acquired the Chippawa battle site in 1995 and preserved 300 acres of it to commemorate the bloody fighting of 1814. Thanks to their foresight and efforts, Chippawa is today among the best-preserved battlefield parks relating to the War of 1812, looking much as it did at the time of the campaign. Although there is some encroachment of housing on the northern side of the battlefield, and a golf course covers part of where the British approached and formed up, there is a wide expanse of the plain remaining, bounded on one side by the river and on the other side by woods, just as it was at the time of the battle. The focal point is a cairn dedicated to those who fought in the battle and to the peace that has prevailed between Canada and the United States over the past two centuries. A self-guided walking tour allows visitors to retrace the events of the battle while a memorial service is held on July 5 each year to commemorate the fallen of all the nations—American, British, Canadian and Native— involved in this pivotal battle.

It seems this recognition of their sacrifice isn't enough to allow the dead to find lasting peace: ghostly soldiers, the violence of phantom warfare and unusual lights startle many visitors to the Chippawa battlefield even today, 200 years later. Accounts from visitors of ghostly activity in the pleasant park setting aren't uncommon. Among the phenomena most commonly reported is people having heard echoes of battle as clearly as if the battle was raging on today. They come away able to describe in vivid detail the chaos and terror of combat. Others have walked the grounds and inexplicably been overcome with feelings of sickness and nausea, or suddenly experienced profound emotional feelings that leave them in tears. Though thankfully rarely, visitors have complained of feeling a heaviness or even outright pain in the chest and head, which they speculate might be a sort of echo of the pain soldiers wounded here 200 years ago would have endured. The Haunted Hamilton paranormal research group conducted an investigation of the site of the battle and caught a swarm of glowing orbs and even some electronic voice phenomena (EVP) on video. Seeing a full body apparition at the Chippawa battlefield is rare, but on occasion spectral soldiers have materialized before startled witnesses.

Encounters with the restless dead at Chippawa date back decades. One of the earliest involved a group of guys who were out on what was then still a farmer's field one night around dusk, firing off rifles for a little fun. This was well before Niagara Parks Commission purchased the battlefield, so it wasn't marked in any way and few people knew the land had any significance. As a result, these guys had no idea where they were, no idea that the land had once seen fierce fighting, no idea that they trod over the graves of fallen soldiers. Only much later did they realize they were target-shooting on what was at one time a battlefield.

The young men set up targets and began honing their marksmanship. They were well away from residential areas, so it seemed at the time like harmless fun. But what these guys couldn't anticipate was that the sounds of the rifles being fired would awaken the spirits of the dead, rousing them from their slumber and causing them to rise up to do battle once more. Just as shadows began to deepen, the young men suddenly heard the sounds of pitched battle all around them. They heard cannons booming, muskets firing, men and horses screaming, orders being bellowed.

At first they assumed that it was just some kind of re-enactment in a fort nearby, but then they realized the battlefield sounds were far too close to be coming from either Fort George or Fort Erie. It sounded like they were right in the midst of the fighting—the rifle fire, the cannons, the yells of desperate and dying men seem to surround them. The longer they listened, the louder and closer the sounds became. The men were terrified; the sounds clearly had no earthly origin. Then the battlefield chorus faded away as quickly as it came, leaving the men dumbstruck and shaking in fear. Target shooting had suddenly lost its appeal and they fled the field.

On another occasion, years later, two men were out hiking around the area. It was about the same time of day—dusk—and they were walking around the battlefield when they heard the same thing, the sounds of battle. Just as with the previous witnesses, the pair heard the sounds of rifle fire and artillery, the shouts of combatants and the screams of the dying. The sounds came out of nowhere, lasted for a few moments and then faded away, leaving the pair standing in the field wondering whether or not to believe their ears.

In preparation for writing the book *Shadows of Niagara: Investigating Canada's Most Haunted Region,* paranormal researcher John Savoie and medium Pauline Raby paid a nighttime visit to the battlefield. Their investigation was particularly fruitful. Right from the start Raby began channeling several spirits who fought and presumably died there in 1814. One entity, that of an 18-year-old American soldier from Maryland named Jeffrey Peters, kept coming through the sensations of battle—the fear, the sounds, the pains of wounds—that threatened to overwhelm the psychic. Historical records do indeed show that a J. Peters was present at the battle.

The spirits didn't just communicate with Raby. On several instances Savoie heard heavy breathing in his ear, as if someone was standing directly behind him, and he distinctly heard someone say hello as soon as they arrived on site. The recorder he carried picked up further spectral voices. Some seemed to be echoes of war, particularly orders given by officers to their soldiers: "Go get them!" or "Ready, fire!" In other instances the voices seemed to be speaking directly to the investigators, such as the one who pleaded, "Go back home." Neither Savoie nor Raby saw any apparitions, but there was little doubt in either one's mind that ethereal regiments were marching across the battlefield, eternally fighting a war that for us has long been confined to the history books.

The most disturbing episode yet reported at Chippawa is also the most recent, occurring in the summer of 2010 and once again taking place around dusk. The eyewitness, a tourist from America with a passion for military history, had spent a few hours wandering the battlefield, reading and photographing the commemorative plaques and trying to visualize how the battle developed over the course of that day so long ago in July of 1814. The sun was just starting to plummet into the west when the man decided to head back to his car.

He had his head down, reviewing images on his digital camera while he walked, when a shape suddenly appeared before him. He looked up quickly, thinking he was about to walk into a tree, and was stunned to find himself standing face to face with a red-coated soldier gripping a musket tightly in his hands. The tourist was about to greet the soldier, who he took for a re-enactor, when the Redcoat suddenly lunged and the long bayonet affixed to the musket drove into his stomach. The American fell to the ground, jerking and writhing, struggling to free himself from the agonizing blade cutting through flesh and bone. He remembers groaning with the pain and that his hands, twisted like claws, tried to grab at the musket to pull the bayonet out. He may have blacked out with the pain because the next thing he remembers he was lying on the grass, completely alone, the soldier long gone. There was no sign of a wound, no blood, only a dull ache that plagued him, on and off, for weeks thereafter.

Phantom soldiers may not be the only ghosts tied to this hallowed ground, however. One report that recently emerged centred upon two employees of Niagara Parks who were involved in transforming what was then empty fields into the park-like setting of today. While on break sitting in a parked car, the men were startled to see the apparition of a Native American suddenly materialize and begin gliding across the battlefield. It moved oddly, almost dancing, as if engaged in some sort of ceremony. Though the spirit was non-threatening, the workers were

frightened and quickly drove away. One of the men—
a 14-year veteran of the Niagara Parks Commission—
apparently tended his resignation that afternoon.

The workers might have expected to see the ghost of
a War of 1812-era soldier, but a Native American? It
actually makes sense based on the historical record, but
few people today would know that during the battle,
American-allied New York Iroquois fought British-allied
Mohawk Iroquois in a forest located on the western borders of the Street farm. They stalked each other noiselessly through the woods before pouncing cat-like upon
their prey. The echoes of gunshots, war-whoops, the clash
of tomahawks and the pitiful screams of the wounded
and dying carried through the trees. It was savage, close-
range combat. Ultimately the New York Iroquois were
victorious and they went about the grim task of slitting
the throats of wounded enemies and gathering scalps.
The carnage within these woods and the emotional toll of
fighting fellow Iroquois drove most of the Natives out
of the war and back to their homes. Maybe the trauma to
the Iroquois psyche was so great that it represents
a wound that has yet to heal. Perhaps that explains
why a restless Iroquois soul might linger even 200 years
after the last scalp was collected.

Based upon the countless testimonials of frightened
eyewitnesses, the Chippawa battlefield is still within the
clutches of its dark and bloody history. Will the tortured
spirits that continue to wage the phantom battle on the
field where they were cut down ever quit the fight? Will
they ever march into the afterlife? Maybe the battlefield
will always retain a somber energy. If a heavy sensation

settles over you while visiting the site, could you be standing on the exact spot where a British or American soldier met his end 200 years ago? It's impossible not to feel the spirits of the dead here.

Who can say for certain if for these dead soldiers the war will ever end? Perhaps years, decades, perhaps even another two centuries from now, the fallen of Chippawa will still be locked in battle.

McFarland House

A spark of fear surfaced in Martha's brown eyes and an icy shiver ran through her body. She stood at the doorway of a bedroom decorated in 19th-century furnishings as chilled, invisible fingers wrapped around her hand. The sensation lasted but a moment. She rubbed her aching hand, numb with a cold not of this world. Members of her tour group looked on expectedly, waiting for her to continue her narration on the history of McFarland House. There were a few bewildered glances among them as they wondered why their guide had halted just outside the room. Martha steadied her shaking nerves and then stepped into the bedroom. Immediately upon crossing the threshold the air sucked from her lungs, leaving her breathless and gasping. More frightened than she cared to admit, she tried to mask her terror from the tourists trailing behind. This supernatural sensation overwhelmed the young guide every time she entered the room, and every time it took her a few seconds to compose herself and shake off the fear so as not to concern her guests.

Martha couldn't explain her breathlessness or the ghostly hand that reached out to her, and it was only in this room that she ever encountered them. But after working at the historic site for a number of years she was certain of one thing: there was something, or someone, in the building besides mortal guides and tourists. While she occasionally experienced the unsettling sensation of being watched by unseen eyes throughout the beautifully restored home, this second floor bedroom was the only room Martha was ever hesitant about entering. Who was the spirit and why was it so strong in this one particular room? Martha came to believe it was the home's original owner, John McFarland, and that the room was the one in which he spent his final days.

Martha isn't alone in believing John McFarland remains behind in his former home, now a museum operated by the Niagara Parks Commission as an example of a residence found in early-19th-century Niagara. Over the years, many people have been left with this certainty after spending some time in the building.

John McFarland was born in Paisley, Scotland, in 1752. He was a widower with four children when he immigrated to Niagara in the early 1790s upon receiving more than 600 acres of land from King George III in reward for his services as a boat-builder to His Majesty's forces. He later purchased additional lots and became one of the largest landholders in the vicinity.

McFarland House offers visitors a glimpse into the past.

McFarland married Margaret Wilson, a widowed neighbour in Niagara-on-the-Lake, and in 1800, with the assistance of his now-adult sons, he built a fine manor to accommodate his growing family. It was a beautiful home, designed to impress friends and reflect his prominent social standing in the young community. McFarland was blessed with five more children with Margaret, and the sounds of their little feet running through the halls brought life to the home and a smile to their father's face.

In the summer of 1812, McFarland must have been a happy man. True, his second wife had passed away a few years prior, but he was surrounded by a loving family, had wealth, was held in high esteem within the community and resided in a fine home. He counted himself lucky to have nine children, to be in good health and to possess bountiful farmland and a profitable brick factory. Life was good for John McFarland, and one can imagine him spending quiet evenings reflecting on how lucky he was.

Then the war erupted. At 60 years of age McFarland was too old for service in the militia, but nonetheless he soon found himself caught up in the conflict. If you lived in Niagara it was impossible to remain untouched by it. The first sign that things had changed was when the British army built a small artillery fort on his property with which to fire on any American boats spotted on the Niagara River. McFarland cheerfully welcomed the youthful soldiers, but inside he was sad because the war suddenly seemed very close, very real.

In the summer of 1813, the war grew closer still. Americans captured Niagara-on-the-Lake and sent the reeling British defenders inland. McFarland did his best not to worry, but he was afraid of what American occupation would mean for him and his family. His prior service to the Crown was well known. Would the invaders target him for persecution?

To distract himself, McFarland threw himself into his work and spent long, tiring days out in the fields. One day, the farmer saw a group of blue-coated American soldiers approaching. They accosted McFarland and his eldest son, James, demanding that they hand over their team of horses. The two men refused and, wielding fence rails as clubs, chased the soldiers off. Shortly thereafter, the soldiers returned in greater numbers to arrest McFarland and his son. They soon found themselves, along with other men of the community, in a prison camp in Green Bush, New York.

To add insult to injury, the Americans threw the McFarland family out of their home and occupied it as a hospital for their sick and wounded. At times, the hall was so filled with dead and injured soldiers that it was almost impossible to reach the upper story without treading on their bodies. Many of these fallen men would never recover from their wounds and died within the home. Their blood stained the wooden floors, the stench of death seeped into the plaster and the dead bodies were buried in unmarked graves somewhere on the property.

When John McFarland was released at the end of the war, he returned to a ruined shell of a home. The roof, all interior wood work (including mouldings, banisters and mantle pieces) and furnishings had been burned for firewood. All personal effects had been either stolen or destroyed. Windows were broken, dried leaves gathered in corners and several seasons of rain and snow had damaged the flooring and walls. The litter of war—bloodied bandages, empty packs, discarded uniforms—lay everywhere. Outside, the paint had begun to weather and peel, and all manner of debris littered the grounds. Neglect had caused the flowers and herbs that had once flourished in gardens to become choked with thick weeds. Untended and overgrown fields completed the sense of loss.

McFarland lost the will to live. His dreams had been shattered. Even after the house was repaired he could not escape his despondency. His family tried to cheer him, but nothing they said or did had any effect on the depression that hovered over him like a black cloud. His children watched as their once robust, cheerful and ambitious father wasted away before their eyes. He retreated into his darkened bedroom in the home he had once been so proud of, and rarely ventured out. As the months passed, his mental and physical health deteriorated further. Less than a year after the war ended, at the age of 63, he died of a broken heart. John McFarland was buried next to his wife in St. Mark's Cemetery.

Today, John McFarland's home is a popular historical museum through which costumed staff members lead groups of eager tourists. Although 200 years have passed and all of his children and their children are dead, McFarland's ghost has never left. His spirit, made restless by the sadness of his final days, did not find peace in death. He clings to his home like mortar, his love for it remaining beyond the grave.

The tragic nature of his death suggested from the beginning that the heartbroken man might not find peace. Local children, avid story-tellers, ghost-hunters and a handful of eyewitnesses continue to build on the legend that McFarland House is heavily haunted. They report unusual lights in the windows after dark, unnatural cold spots and chilly breezes without an identifiable source, and mysterious hushed voices and footsteps in the lower part of the home.

John McFarland is a melancholy ghost, a lost soul. He would undoubtedly prefer to be reunited with his family on the other side, yet he remains anchored to the mortal plane by the sadness that weighed down his spirit during the final days of his life. Those few who have seen him suggest that he wanders up and down the hallways and throughout the finely furnished rooms, often pausing to gaze mournfully out a window at a world he no longer recognizes.

"I saw a tall, elderly-looking man wearing what seemed to be a period costume, so I assumed he was a staff member," relates a woman who had an unusual experience during a visit to McFarland House. "He was reaching out to the mantle above the fireplace, as if placing something there. I only saw him from the back, and only for a moment, before turning my attention back to the tour group. When I glanced back again a second or two later the old man was gone. It happened too fast for him to have walked through the other door. It was as if he just vanished. But he must have been there because crystal ornaments that rest on the mantle were tinkling ever so slightly, as if rustled by the wind." This woman was left convinced that she had seen, if only momentarily, the ghost of John McFarland himself.

A tour through McFarland House may include a ghostly encounter with its original owner.

McFarland may not be alone in his beautifully restored home. Visitors and staff alike believe that there may be several ghosts in residence, including ethereal soldiers and a maid who takes dedication and service to a whole new level.

American soldiers have been spotted wandering through the building and its surrounding grounds. Presumably, these men died here during the period in which the home served as a U.S. Army field hospital and may even be among those who are believed to lie in unmarked graves somewhere on the property. How McFarland coexists with the very men who were responsible for the ruination of his home and his own spiritual downfall is a mystery. It must be a tense relationship to say the least.

The truth is, we have no idea exactly how many men died in the home, or where they are buried. Even Rebecca Pascoe, manager-curator of the site, doesn't have these answers. "I'm afraid that I cannot absolutely confirm or deny this ghostly tale," she told us honestly. "However, since the house was being used as a military hospital and logic would dictate that not all patients survived their wounds, then yes, it is possible that soldiers died here and are in fact buried on the property."

Those who have encountered these blue-coated spirits need no documentary proof to tell them that one or more American soldiers continue to occupy the building and the grounds just as they did throughout 1813. The involuntary shiver every time they recall their haunting experience is all the evidence they need. These undead men-at-arms reach out from beyond the grave to ensure we don't forget that they lie beneath the grass where children play and families enjoy picnics. Some people claim they appear in good health, tall and straight-backed, muskets at the ready, while others witness only bloodied and battle-weary soldiers.

One witness heard terrifying moans of pain emanating from within the house during the off-season when the building is closed, while a medium who explored the building had sudden insight that made her certain that three people had been buried near the front wall in the basement and that perhaps five others were buried on the grounds. Jack Colgan was a young boy when he visited McFarland House and saw one of these soldierly spooks, a figure he remembers today as a manifestation of somber gloom. During the course of the guided tour, his eyes wandered back to the room the group had just left. There, standing grim and silent, was a cadaverous man in uniform with an angry glow flickering through the sockets of his eyes. In the time it took Jack to blink, the vision was gone. But the fear that gripped the young boy wouldn't dissolve so quickly. Almost two decades later, he is still unnerved by the memory.

While the apparitions of long-dead soldiers elicit shudders of horror, the presence of the McFarlands' former servant is more comforting. It's this spirit that staff members are most familiar with, and they've grown accustomed to her occasional antics.

The McFarlands were wealthy enough that they would have had several servants. A head cook, a head housekeeper and a head butler resided within the home, augmented by numerous day staff—younger men and women who lived nearby. Senior domestics in a wealthy, established home like the McFarlands' were valuable, trusted staff. Some servants remained with the same family for decades, becoming as much a part of the household as the family members. Between 1875 and 1943, when the last remaining members of the family left the home, dozens of people would have worked in the home, and some would have served long enough to perhaps leave a permanent mark in the building's aged wood.

"Although we have not yet uncovered any historic resources regarding exactly who the McFarlands' servants were, over time we've gotten a sense of who one of them might be. She's been described by mediums as older, so old that were you to suddenly see her in a mirror she might frighten you—but don't be afraid. She's just been here for a while," explains Rebecca, noting that the spectral servant is as harmless as she is venerable. "There's talk that her name is Betsey and that she wears a white cap on her head. Both are fitting details; Betsey was a common appellation that mistresses sometimes universally called their serving staff regardless of the employees' actual names, and female domestics until the Edwardian age typically did wear some type of decorative indoor hair covering like mobcaps or kerchiefs."

Current staff members, while occasionally confused or even startled by Betsey's presence, have generally learned to co-exist with her. But they have the benefit of working in the daylight, with bright sunlight streaming through windows and a steady stream of visitors through the door. The same cannot be said of those who watch over the house at night.

Constables working for the Niagara Parks Commission are responsible for maintaining overnight security along a long stretch of the Niagara Parkway at numerous historic sites and natural parks. A night walk down by the falls, where it is always bright and lively even in the witching hours, is quite a different thing than being posted at McFarland House. Set in a rambling park, during the day the house is the absolute embodiment of quaint Georgian elegance. At night, though, the property takes on a different air. Sometimes everything is fine; nothing feels any different after dark than during a bright, sunny afternoon. But there are other times when you get the distinct impression that you may not be the only one in the house. Many night-duty constables assigned to McFarland House have had the sensation that the house was not empty, even though the doors were locked tight and the rooms were pitch-black.

Some constables have even seen a woman—Betsey—keeping her watch. Above the main entrance, in what was once the servants' quarters, there is a window with a recessed place to sit. It's the perfect spot to watch all the comings and goings of the home. From here, servants in years past could see who was coming down the lane to visit the McFarlands, who might be passing by on the road out front, and perhaps even spying to see whether the master and mistress of the house were leaving so that they might sneak a moment for themselves. It was, and remains today, the perfect vantage point for keeping watch over one's domain. Perhaps that's why Betsey chooses to watch out this window, curiously gazing out onto a world that is alien to her.

All of McFarland House's windows have cream linen curtains that are drawn shut when the staff leaves for the day. Niagara Parks constables claim that some nights, as they come up the walkway, with the house locked tight and all its security alarms functioning, they see the curtains in the upper window part, and the outline of someone watching appears. "There are staff on our force of constables who have been officers for decades, individuals with nerves of steel who have served across numerous forces and seen things that would jar the sensibilities of many of the rest of us," says Rebecca. "And yet they admit to seeing someone standing above, quietly helping to keep the evening watch. I like to think it's Betsey."

Over the course of 2011 in preparation for the War of 1812 bicentennial celebrations, McFarland House was fortunate enough to be part of a large capital investment project, the biggest undertaking of its kind since the house opened to the public in 1959. It was exciting for the staff, but there was some trepidation as well. "Going into the reno we all wondered what might happen after all the disruptions to this important historic building," remembers Rebecca. "Would those who shared our space be perturbed by the construction, the noise and all the changes? Would they welcome them? Or would they even notice? We weren't sure what to expect—or which alternative we really hoped for."

The renovations took place in the back wing, which was built in 1875 to create extra living space on the ground floor for the growing McFarland family, and servants' quarters on the second floor. When the Niagara Parks Commission took over the property in the 1950s they altered the original rooms. On the ground floor, a snack bar and retail area occupied the space where the back parlour once stood, and public washrooms were installed in the space occupied by the old kitchen. Upstairs saw even more radical changes. A small staircase running directly from the kitchen up into the servants' quarters was removed, and the bedrooms on the second floor were significantly altered so they could be made part of a cramped curator's apartment that was shoe-horned into the space.

The 2011 renovations brought the wing back to its original floor plan. The 1950s apartment upstairs was taken out and the old washrooms downstairs were demolished. In their place are now staff rooms and offices based on the historic room placements and a bright, shiny new kitchen where modern appliances and stainless steel countertops take the place of the brick hearth, dry sinks and wooden work tables that came before. This new kitchen became the scene of harmless but perplexing activity that caused staff to question whether resident spirits were making their feelings about the renovations known.

"Although we had a few initial hiccups with some of our new appliances, one by one these supposedly unexplainable idiosyncrasies were solved. All it took was adjusting a setting here, being more careful to avoid hitting a reset button there, and everything was set right. Except for one thing: the oven," explains Rebecca. "Our brand new, top of the line oven was installed on the exact spot where a half beehive oven once stood. Indeed, during the renovations the 1875 hearth lintel was uncovered. Despite consulting with every sales rep and repairman involved in the selection, purchase, delivery, installation and servicing of our new oven, it has an unexpected tendency to alert us to timers we have not set."

As the first person to come in each day, it was Rebecca's job to sweep through the building, turning on lights and appliances as she went. Since they bake all the cookies, biscuits and scones for their historic tearoom themselves, this routine also included warming up the oven. For about the first two months after the renovations, at least twice a week she would find herself running down from her upstairs office to the kitchen below, alarmed by the frantic, impossible-to-ignore oven timer. Initially, she thought it was merely a useful alert that the oven had reached the preset temperature. Not so. Once she talked to her coworkers, Rebecca discovered that the alarm didn't sound every time you turned on the oven, so it clearly wasn't a helpful temperature alert. They had no idea what it was, nor could they explain why it would suddenly go off. There seemed to be no rational explanation.

Soon, it was happening even when people were in the room. "Inexplicably, you can be standing at one counter mixing cake batter, the oven timer turned completely off, and all of a sudden the dial will jump on its own accord," continues Rebecca. "We've noticed it jump forward five or 10 minutes at a time, or sometimes change to run fully counter-clockwise past zero and settle back at 55 minutes. Even once we started keeping close watch over the appliance, someone continued to play with the timer dial—you could unfailingly look up from your work every few minutes to check that it was firmly set to zero, but watch out: pay full attention to something else for even a few moments and it will skip. I can't figure it out. Is someone playing pranks on us? Or are they remembering baking of their own that must be attended to?"

The staff at McFarland House is united in believing Betsey must be responsible for the strange activity. It makes sense, when one stops to think about it. Who else but a domestic would be so attached to a kitchen?

Danielle Lamoureux, a long-time staffer at McFarland House, discovered the spiritual forces within the building in an unusual fashion and over the span of months. Danielle always thought there was something strange about the upstairs door that separates the original 1800 front wing from the 1875 servants' quarters addition, which today houses the staff area. Usually this door is so stiff that you have to push hard to get it open. It's rarely used. Every once in a while, though, Danielle would climb the back stairs and watch as the latch of the door would skip and the door slowly swing open in front of her. There was never anyone there. The door was opening on its own.

"I honestly didn't think overly much about it at the time; it was just something that would happen," Danielle remembers. "I would close the door on my way past and carry on with my day. It was only when one of my coworkers mentioned that it happened to her too and I agreed that it was a fairly normal occurrence that I realized it wasn't normal at all." Danielle began to conclude that a door swinging open by itself was, by definition, paranormal.

Although she had seen the door open on its own many times, one episode in particular was unsettling. The day was suitably atmospheric. Angry black clouds loomed overhead, crowding out the sun and dimming the landscape below. Thunder rumbled. Rain pounded heavily on the roof and ran in rivers off the eaves. It was miserable and moody, the perfect day for a ghost story.

"It was during the summer when our tearoom wasn't open due to renovations, so we only had to worry about the gift shop and the tours. We typically only had four staff members in on a Monday, but this day was even worse because we had lost one staffer to illness and one to meetings, so there were only two of us at the shop," remembers Danielle. "This would have been fine if it had been a typical Monday. As it was, we ended up getting six tours one after the other, so I would come off a tour just as my fellow interpreter would start one and vice versa."

Because McFarland House has little electrical lighting and there was little natural illumination owing to the grey weather, the rooms through which the tours passed that day were filled with dark shadows. The dimness limited the public's appreciation and made conditions unsafe, so as soon as Danielle had a free moment she ran through the house lighting candles on the main floor while her coworker was outside starting the next tour.

With the first floor lit up, Danielle took a handful of candles upstairs to illuminate the remainder of the building. She lined them up just inside the staff room. Her plan was to light them in a row and then run them inside the front wing, hopefully before she heard anyone enter the gift shop downstairs and before her coworker brought her tour up to the second floor. Things didn't go according to plan, however.

"I had just started lighting the candles when the door to the 1800 wing swung open behind me. I turned around and closed it, making sure it was firmly latched this time. I didn't want the tour to come up the stairway and accidentally see all the way into our modern staff room in the addition. I was in a bit of a rush so I quickly returned to my candles, only to have the door swing open behind me again the second my back was turned. This happened three times—I would close the door, make sure the latch was down, and the instant I had turned my back it would open again. Finally I got fed up, and the last time I closed the partition I told the door to stop it in a very stern voice. Then I turned back to the candles and nothing happened. I got the candles lit and into the house, and nothing else happened for the rest of the day," recalls Danielle.

Since the upstairs staff rooms were historically the living quarters of senior domestic servants, and since it would have been unheard of for a member of the family to enter the servant's wing, Danielle believes Betsey was responsible for the heavy door swinging open as if by an invisible hand. The presence of a ghostly servant working unseen alongside her doesn't concern the long-time employee, however. She's gotten used to it, and considers the presence of spirits part of the historic building's charm.

Rebecca Pascoe agrees wholeheartedly: "Personally, I find it comforting. I like to think that perhaps there's another woman looking over my shoulder, keeping me company in the kitchen, helping me not to forget to keep watch over the biscuits in the oven."

Thousands of people visit the beautifully restored McFarland House every year. They enjoy the experience of stepping back in time to an era when our nation was young, and through a guided tour learn the fascinating history of the building and the people associated with it. Many of them linger to sample refreshments at the McFarland Tea Garden. Only a tiny handful of those who visit this living history museum ever experiences anything unusual or paranormal. And yet for many people, the possibility that one might make an intimate connection with the past by seeing or sensing a ghost—whether it's John McFarland himself, the eternally devoted Betsey or an obscure American soldier—seems to add to the building's charm. If you find yourself in Niagara, be sure to visit McFarland House and see for yourself. John McFarland is a hospitable man and will surely welcome you into his home.

Acknowledgements

The completion of this book would have been impossible without the support, dedication, and selfless efforts of more people than it is possible to properly credit. Therefore, we must restrict ourselves to naming but a few.

First and foremost, we'd like to thank the dedicated staff members of the museums, archives, libraries and historical societies that we turned to while researching this book, who cheerfully assisted our searches for details on hauntings and sometimes revealed previously unknown ghost stories that we could include.

We'd like to draw attention to a few individuals and organizations that stood out in graciously lending their time and expertise: Rebecca Pascoe, manager/curator of McFarland House, who generously compiled ghost stories from staff members on our account; Kyle Upton of Niagara Ghost Tours and the author of *Niagara Ghosts* volumes I and II, most particularly for providing additional details on the Fort George hauntings; Daniel Cumerlato of Haunted Hamilton, who runs guided ghost tours through Niagara-on-the-Lake; Ron Dale of the Niagara Parks Commission and an authority on the War of 1812, for setting the historical record straight; Melissa Bottomley, manager/curator of the Laura Secord Homestead, who shed light on this true Canadian heroine; the Sippican Historical Society; Sheila Gibbs, author of *Ghosts of Chatham-Kent* volumes I and II, and guide for Chatham Ghost Tours, for going the extra mile to assist us; the staff of the Olde Angel Inn, always helpful; and Heather Gorham, manager/curator at Old Fort Erie.

We'd like to thank Nancy Foulds at Ghost House Books for embracing this book from the start, and the guidance and support she provided along the way. Working with Nancy is a true pleasure. Thanks also to the unsung creative team at Lone Pine Publishing for turning this idea into a reality and making it pleasing to look at.

And of course, we have to thank all those individuals who came forward with their own personal brushes with the supernatural. It takes a lot of courage to open up about experiences that are often emotionally charged, and to risk the possibility of ridicule or disbelief while doing so. This book is the richer for each individual who took this leap and entrusted us with their stories. We thank them all.

Personal Acknowledgements

Andrew Hind writes: I'd like to draw attention to the historical re-enactors and staff at historical sites and museums for their tireless and often unheralded work in keeping the history of the War of 1812 alive and presenting it in an interesting manner.

In addition, I want to thank Maria for taking a trip with me 200 years into the past to explore the otherworldly aspects of the War of 1812. She made this journey despite enduring a lot in her personal life at the time, which makes my appreciation of her contributions, her companionship and her friendship all the greater. Remember Maria, it's not the challenges that define us, but rather how we face them.

About the Authors

Maria Da Silva and Andrew Hind are freelance writers who specialize in the paranormal, history and travel. They have a passion for bringing to light unusual stories, chilling tales of the supernatural, little-known episodes in history and fascinating locations few people know about. Together, they have contributed numerous articles to magazine publications and newspapers, including the *Toronto Star*, *Lakeland Boating*, *Horizons*, *Canada's History*, *Muskoka Magazine*, *History Magazine* and regular features in *Paranormal Magazine*. They also conduct guided historical and ghost tours that help people connect with the past in a personal way, and speak freely at public forums about their work and passion. This is their third book in the Ghost House Books series; their preceding titles are *Cottage Country Ghosts* and *More Ontario Ghost Stories*.

Maria has always been fascinated by ghosts and the paranormal, and regularly explores the subject through her writing. Andrew developed a love of history early on, and he hopes, through his books with Maria, to develop a similar passion in others. He has a special interest in military history. *Ghost Stories of the War of 1812* is Maria and Andrew's twelfth book together, and their fourth for Lone Pine Publishing. They are currently working on a sequel to *Cottage Country Ghosts*, which will see them explore the haunted heritage of Haliburton, the Kawarthas, Muskoka, Georgian Bay and the Near-North.

Maria and Andrew reside in Bradford, Ontario.